The Eye of the Crocodile

The Eye of the Crocodile

Val Plumwood

Edited by Lorraine Shannon

Australian
National
University

E PRESS

Published by ANU E Press
The Australian National University
Canberra ACT 0200, Australia
Email: anuepress@anu.edu.au
This title is also available online at http://epress.anu.edu.au

---

National Library of Australia Cataloguing-in-Publication entry

Author: Plumwood, Val.

Title: The Eye of the crocodile / Val Plumwood ; edited by
                  Lorraine Shannon.

ISBN: 9781922144164 (pbk.) 9781922144171 (ebook)

Notes   Includes bibliographical references and index.

Subjects: Predation (Biology)
                  Philosophy of nature.

Other Authors/Contributors:
                  Shannon, Lorraine.

Dewey Number: 591.53

Cover design and layout by ANU E Press

Cover image supplied by Mary Montague of Montague Leong Designs Pty Ltd.
http://www.montagueleong.com.au

Printed by Griffin Press

This edition © 2012 ANU E Press

Contents

Acknowledgements

The editor wishes to thank the following for permission to use previously published material:

A version of Chapter One was published as 'Being Prey' in *Terra Nova*, Vol. 1, No. 3 Summer, 1996, pp. 32-44.

'Animals and Ecology: Towards a Better Integration' reprinted by permission of *Food for Thought*, ed. S. Sapontzis, Prometheus Books, New York, 2004, pp. 344-358.

'Tasteless' reprinted by permission of *Environmental Values*, Vol. 17, Issue 3, 2008, pp. 323-330.

The publisher acknowledges the grateful assistance of Dr. Denise Russell, editor of *Animal Issues*, for permission to reproduce material post-publication:

'Biribi, in Memoriam: A Wombat Wake' reprinted by permission of *Animal Issues*, Vol. 4, No. 1, 2000, pp. 21-29 and 'Babe, the Tale of the Speaking Meat' in *Animal Issues*, Vol. 1, No. 1, 1997, pp. 21-35 and Vol. 1, No. 2, 1997, pp. 21-30.

Preface

The late Val Plumwood was a feminist writer and scholar, the author of three books and over 80 published papers. Her major books, *Feminism and the mastery of nature*, and *Environmental culture: The crisis of reason* published by Routledge, London, in December 1993, were major contributions to feminist and environmental philosophy. Having deliberated profoundly on her experience of surviving a crocodile attack in February 1985 in Australia's magnificent Kakadu National Park (the setting of Crocodile Dundee, filmed there a few months after the attack), Val Plumwood was equipped to write an account which is much more than an adventure story, one which addresses the meaning of our lives and major philosophical issues of our time. Unfortunately this account was unfinished at the time of her death and *The Eye of the Crocodile* combines the three completed chapters of this book with earlier writings on the themes of animals, death and predation.

Val understood the crocodile as it was seen in both Indigenous Australian and ancient Egyptian narrative, as a trickster figure, a deliverer of judgement on the errant human. In biblical metaphor, the crocodile delivers adverse judgement on human pretensions to master a malleable world. The crocodile is now one of the last remaining major predators of human beings, a creature which perceives us not in the inflated terms in which we tend to view ourselves, as cyber-masters or techno-gods transcending the merely animal realm, but simply as another palatable item of food. Crocodile predation on humans still has a unique ability to recall to us something uncomfortable and unflattering about who we are, to teach a lesson from the past we forget at our peril about the unconquerability of the world we think we master.

These opening tense chapters are a story of struggle and survival set in the powerful landscape of Australia's Top End. As a feminist writer and environmental philosopher Val Plumwood looked into the eye of the crocodile and reflected on the meaning of her experience of being crocodile prey. This was an experience which changed her view of selfhood, human life and human freedom. The master story of Western culture places at the centre of the human story an invulnerable, heroic rational consciousness, struggling to reduce the energy, excess and otherness of nature to a humanised and moralised order which will do his bidding and reflect back his own conception of his deserts. Val Plumwood shows how the crocodile as trickster can help us reshape the old human-centred master narrative into a more modest tale appropriate for new times.

Few people have survived three death rolls from the Saltwater Crocodile, perhaps the most formidable remaining predator of humans, and lived to tell the tale.

The Eye of the Crocodile is not only a survival tale, but a unique reflection on the meaning of human identity, human struggle and human death from a narrator who was also a major environmental philosopher.

Introduction

Freya Mathews, Kate Rigby, Deborah Rose

Val Plumwood was one the great philosophers, activists, feminists, teachers, and everyday naturalists of the late 20th and early 21st centuries. In the course of her productive life she wrote two great philosophical monographs which became key texts in the emerging fields of environmental philosophy and ecofeminism. Her stature as a thinker of power and influence was reflected in the fact that she was included in the 2001 book *50 Key Thinkers on the Environment*[1] along with luminaries such as Buddha, Gandhi, and Arne Naess. Val died of a stroke in 2008 at the age of 68. She was not only an influential environmental thinker, whose book *Feminism and the mastery of nature* has become a classic of environmental philosophy; she was also a woman who fearlessly lived life on her own deeply considered terms, often in opposition to prevailing norms.

Val's philosophy had its origins in, and vigorously contributed to, a pivotal moment in Western thought. In the 1970s a radical critique of traditional Western conceptions of nature emerged simultaneously at opposite ends of the Western world, in Australia and in Norway. The Norwegian critique emanated from philosopher, Arne Naess, who became the founder of the deep ecology movement. The less well-known but just as trenchant Australian critique emanated from a small group of philosophers centred on The Australian National University in Canberra. Val, who was then known as Val Routley, and her partner, Richard Routley (later to become Richard Sylvan) were key members of this group. They, like Arne Naess, recognised that the environmental problems that were coming into view at that time were the result not merely of faulty policies and technologies but of underlying attitudes to the natural world that were built into the very foundations of Western thought. According to the Routleys, these attitudes were the expression of *human chauvinism*, the groundless belief, amounting to nothing more than prejudice, that only human beings mattered, morally speaking; to the extent that anything else mattered at all, according to this attitude, it mattered only because it had some kind of utility for us. Together the Routleys challenged this assumption; together they posed the pivotal question, 'is there a need for a new, an environmental, ethic', an ethic of nature?[2]

---

1   J. Palmer, ed. *50 Key Thinkers on the Environment*, London, Routledge, 2001.
2   Richard Routley, 'Is there a need for new, an environmental ethic?' *Sophia*, Vol. 1 (proceedings of the 15th World Congress of Philosophy, 1973). Although the original paper was published in Richard's name, it was greatly elaborated by Richard and Val jointly, and re-published several years later, as 'Human chauvinism and environmental ethics,' in Don Mannison, Michael McRobbie and Richard Routley, eds, *Environmental Philosophy*, Canberra, The Australian National University, 1982.

The questions the Routleys and their colleagues unearthed and tackled in the 1970s were questions that would help to set the agenda for environmental philosophy. In those early days they were mainly writing for other philosophers, and being logicians as well as environmental thinkers, their papers drew heavily on the vocabulary of logical and semantic theory. This background in logic gave both the Routleys prodigious intellectual muscle, and later, in *Feminism and the mastery of nature*, Val was to turn her training in logical theory to advantage with her impressive analysis of the logic of dualistic thinking. But the technical register of the early writing also meant that, unlike Naess' deep ecology, the Routleys' version of radical environmentalism failed to gain the currency it deserved outside the academy.

However, the Routleys were forest activists as well as philosophers, and in 1975 they published a seminal activist book which did reach a more general audience. This was *The fight for the forests*, a comprehensive economic, scientific, socio-political and philosophical critique of the Australian forestry industry. As David Orton pointed out in a memorial essay on Richard Sylvan after Sylvan's death in 1996, the book was pioneering not only in its comprehensive approach to an environmental issue, but in its insistence that the most fundamental conflicts in forestry were over values, not facts.[3]

During the 1970s, Val and Richard built a remote stone house in a rainforest on Plumwood Mountain south of Canberra. They constructed the house themselves, out of stones found on the property, and as they built they also wrote some of the key articles which were to shape environmental philosophy. The amazingly creative Routley partnership broke up in the early 1980s, and divorce followed. Val stayed on at the mountain, taking the name of the magnificent plumwood tree that was the signature species of the local rainforest ecosystem. (It was at this time that Richard also changed his name to Sylvan.) It remained important to Val to live the ecological values she was dedicated to theorising, the 'thinking' flowing naturally from 'building' and 'dwelling' in the heart of her mountain, as Heidegger might have put it.

The question that continued to preoccupy Val throughout this period was that of anthropocentrism. Along with others, she saw that anthropocentrism, as a value system, rests on the assumption that there is a categorical distinction between humanity and nature: human beings are endowed with something the rest of nature lacks. This 'something' is of course assumed to be mind. Just like plants and animals and rocks, we are made of matter, but in addition to our material bodies, we possess minds, and minds are somehow categorically different from bodies and superior to them. Underlying the conceptual division between humanity and nature then, is a deep conceptual opposition between mind and

---

3   D. Orton, 'In memory of Richard Sylvan,' *The Trumpeter*, Vol. 14 No. 1, 1997.

matter, which becomes refined, in the Western tradition, into an opposition between reason and nature. In her doctoral thesis, which was published in 1992 as *Feminism and the mastery of nature*, Val provided a comprehensive analysis of how this division between reason and nature had historically been constructed and how it informs many of the ongoing foundational categories of Western thought. Hers was by no means the first analysis of such *dualism*, or binary thinking; but it was the most comprehensive within the environmental literature. She showed brilliantly how this dualistic system of thought created value hierarchies that systematically rendered inferior all the terms that came to be associated with nature rather than reason: women, the working class, the colonised, the Indigenous, as well as the other-than-human world. She thereby demonstrated that the ideology underpinning the domination of nature in the contemporary West is simultaneously an ideology legitimating and naturalising the domination of many subjugated social groups. The implication was that environmentalism and struggles for social justice cannot be separated out from one another. Moreover, as long as the assumptions underlying our social and environmental thinking remain unexamined, these pervasive patterns of oppression will remain inescapable. We need new understandings of the human and of nature that close the conceptual gulf between them. This means putting mind back into matter: restoring intelligence to body, and agency to nature.

In her book, *Environmental culture* (2002), Val elaborated her original analysis of dualism, and especially of reason, and applied this analytical framework in an up-to-the-minute way to questions of science, politics, economics, ethics, spirituality and ecology itself. She argued for a form of ecological rationality that would replace the instrumentalising rationalism that has characterised the Western tradition and that has reached its apogee in the modernity of the contemporary global market. After this book, Val began writing essays that increasingly drew stories into philosophical argument. Having developed a powerful analytic framework, she wanted to find ways to continue to communicate her life's passion, and to have an impact on readers outside the academic world. As she wrote in her beautiful essay 'Journey to the Heart of Stone', 'creative writing can also play an important part by making visible new possibilities for radically open and non-reductive ways to experience the world.'[4]

Clearly, Val had come to believe that diagnosing the problems was not enough. It had been decades since she and Richard had asked that crucial question: is there a need for a new, an environmental, ethic? In turning toward the imagination, and the creative, she was making a cultural and political point: 'If our species does not survive the ecological crisis, it will probably be due to our failure to

---

4   Val Plumwood, 'Journey to the heart of stone,' in *Culture, creativity and environment: New environmentalist criticism*, eds. F. Beckett and T. Gifford, Amsterdam, Rodopi, 2007, p. 17.

imagine and work out new ways to live with the earth, to rework ourselves and our high energy, high-consumption, and hyper-instrumental societies adaptively. The time of *Homo reflectus*, the self-critical and self-revising one, has surely come. *Homo faber*, the thoughtless tinkerer, is clearly not going to make it. We will go onwards in a different mode of humanity, or not at all.'[5] Along with her continuing work as a forest activist, she was making a turn toward stories in her writing, and developing an interest in the new field of ecologically oriented literary and cultural studies, or ecocriticism. In 2002, she was invited to present a keynote lecture at the biannual conference of the Association for the Study of Literature and Environment (UK), which led her to venture into a more lyrical mode of philosophical writing, as can be seen from her beautiful homage to stone in the volume that arose from this gathering (2007). In her words, 'writers are amongst the foremost of those who can help us to think differently'; by writers she meant story-tellers, poets, and other creative communicators who could produce enlivened or re-animated accounts of the agency and creativity of nature.[6]

Although, in her later writing, Val was beginning to relate her philosophical reflections more explicitly to salient personal experiences, she was dismissive of the idea that she should write a memoir of her own life. It was clear to those who were close to her, however, that she had been no stranger to hardship and heartbreak. Val was born on the eve of World War II into a relatively poor, but well-educated family living on a small land grant at the edge of Sydney. Her mother home-schooled her for a while, which allowed her plenty of time to explore the local bushland and bond with the family's chooks, the sale of whose eggs supplemented her father's meagre income. Subsequently excelling at school, she received a scholarship to study at Sydney University, where she majored in Philosophy, graduating with First Class Honours in 1965. During this time, she fell pregnant to a fellow student, John Macrae, whom she subsequently married. Their son was born in 1958, and a daughter followed in 1960. However, the emotional and financial difficulties of supporting two small children was overwhelming for two such young parents, and Val felt obliged to give up their baby girl for adoption in order to continue with her studies. Tragically, their daughter, whom they had already lost once, was murdered in her teens, while their son died of a degenerative illness in his 20s. Although she never wrote about the pain of these terrible losses, she has described her struggle to maintain the little rural cemetery in which her son is buried as a place where death can be folded back into life by allowing native vegetation to flourish on and around the graves.[7]

---

5 Val Plumwood, 'Review of Deborah Bird Rose's *Reports from a wild country*,' *Australian humanities review*, Vol. 42, 2007.

6 Val Plumwood, 'Nature in the active voice,' *Australian humanities review*, Vol. 46, 2009, pp. 113-129.

7 Val Plumwood, 'The cemetery wars: Cemeteries, biodiversity and the sacred,' *Local-Global: identity, security and community*, Vol. 3. Special issue: Exploring the legacy of Judith Wright, eds. Martin Mulligan and Yaso Nadarajah, 2007, pp. 54-71.

One of the most famous events in her life was the crocodile attack that occurred in 1985, and it was this event that she was writing about when she died. While kayaking alone in Kakadu National Park in northern Australia at the onset of the Wet season, she was seized by a large crocodile, and death-rolled not once, but three times. (Crocodiles drown their prey by holding them under water.) Unaccountably released from the croc's jaws after the third roll, she crawled for hours, with appalling injuries and stunning courage, through tropical swamps, never far from further crocodiles, in search of safety. Eventually, somewhat miraculously, she was rescued, by a park ranger. This epic experience of course made her uniquely credentialed, as an environmental thinker, to write about death and its place in nature, and she proceeded to do this in a series of beautiful and widely read essays, on the human as prey and as food for nature. She was much preoccupied in latter years with re-visioning death and revising, in appropriately ecological terms, the rituals that accompany it in our society.

The essays included in this book are divided into three sections: the first three comprise the beginning of the book she was working on at the time of her death. Arising from her own near-death experience in Kakadu, these chapters are specifically concerned with crocodile predation on humans, where this phenomenon recalls to us, Val argues, something uncomfortable and unflattering about who we are, teaching us a lesson from the past we forget at our peril about the resistant agency of the material world we think we master. We expect this world to do our bidding and conform to a human conception of our rights, but, as Val shows, the crocodile can help us reshape this old human-centred master narrative into a more modest tale appropriate for new times.

The essays included in the second section address nonhuman animals, and express Val's growing interest in the complex lives of nonhumans and the kinds of questions we face when we regard nonhuman others as sentient agents, perhaps even kin. The first examines human grief at the death of a wild wombat and celebrates the author's relationship with this native animal. The second takes the film *Babe* as an example of how a work of representation can pose many ethico-political questions that lie at the heart of human-animal relations.

The third section opens with an essay which provides an excellent introduction to Val's thinking over the last few years of her life on the relationship between humans and animals. It focuses on the treatment of farm animals and advocates an ecological animalism which supports and celebrates animals and encourages a dialogical ethics of sharing and negotiation or partnership between humans and animals. The final chapter interweaves the crocodile story with the story of the 'cemetery wars'[8] in an endeavour to rethink the ways in which our culture deals with death, including, and especially, the materiality of the corpse. These

---

8   Val Plumwood, 'The cemetery wars', *Local-Global*.

two narratives are linked by seeing life as being in circulation and they suggest that mortuary practices might affirm death as an opportunity of life for others in the ecological community. As this chapter contains a significant amount of repetition from earlier chapters, we decided to publish an abridged version as the material on death and particularly the material on Val's son's burial place seemed an appropriate place to draw the book to a close.

Val's visionary preoccupation with the question of death in the final years of her life was honoured after her own death by the impromptu circle of friends and associates who spontaneously came together into a kind of informal 'friends of Val' group to arrange her funeral and put her affairs in order. Overcoming huge bureaucratic and practical obstacles, members of this little group managed to obtain a permit for a home burial on Plumwood Mountain. Val was duly and reverently laid to rest, with full-flight ecological poetics, in the beautiful garden she had established around the house she had built with her own hands out of the rock of the mountain. Even in her death then, she led by her ecological example.[9]

Acknowledgement

Sections of this introduction have been adapted from F. Mathews, 'Vale Val,' *Environmental values,* Vol. 17, 2008, pp. 317-321.

---

9   Accounts of the burial, as well as tributes and discussions, can be found on a web site that has been set up to honour Val's memory, <http://valplumwood.com>

First section

1. Meeting the predator

Try to look a crocodile in that eye hovering just above the waterline of the swamp. Do you detect recognition of your humanity there? You are a matter of indifference to it when it is full, a prey to be devoured when it is hungry. The eye of the crocodile is a Jobian metaphor for the world, not the only one, but one, perhaps that deserves more attention from those who demand that 'god' or 'nature' be designed for them and them alone.

William E. Connolly, 'Voices from the whirlwind' in Jane Bennett and William Chaloupka eds. *In the nature of things* (Minneapolis, University of Minnesota Press, 1993, p. 205).

No matter how long the log lies in the river, it will never become a crocodile.

African Proverb

My story begins and ends in tropical northern Australia, in the Stone Country of Arnhem Land. This is a land of stone sculpted by sky, wind and water to immense, fantastic forms. The abrasive power of the dry season winds is matched by the erosive power of the wet season storms whose rains pound the land from December to April.

Shrouded stone figures and great sandstone heads gaze out over country formed by a thousand million years of vigorous marital struggle between mother earth and father sky. The energy of that struggle, amorous perhaps as well as abrasive, between the sandstone sheet and the hot, hyperactive atmosphere, has ground the great stone plateau into strange, maze-like ruins, ever-new disclosures of the infinite variety of the earth narrative that is weathered stone.

Stone, wind and water in collaboration shape this land. The power of the Stone Country is manifest in the estuary below, in the extreme annual flooding so crucial for the ecology of the Kakadu region. For the human cultures who lived in the fertile estuary of the East Alligator and other rivers fed by the Stone Country, cultures that had a deeply nourishing relationship with their country, it was a place abundant in food and natural beauty, but where the human had to situate itself in relation to many other powerful forces and elements. It is Ngalyod, the Rainbow Serpent, who holds the power of water, the key to life in this environment. Her water cycles are majestic and creative. As the wet season rainbow arches across the sky, Ngalyod recycles life in this place and performs the yearly integration of land, sky and water.

***

I suppose I have always been the sort of person who 'goes too far'. I certainly went much too far that torrential wet season day in February 1985 when I paddled my little red canoe to the point where the East Alligator River surges out of the Stone Country of the Arnhem Land Plateau. It was the wrong place to be on the first day of the monsoon, when Lightning Man throws the rainbow across the sky and heavy rains begin to lash the land. The rains, pouring off thousands of square miles of sandstone plateau, unleash huge seasonal floods that sweep downriver and submerge for the next half-year the low-lying country on the flood-plain below. It was in this place, as the gushing rain squalls reunited earth and sky, I had a close encounter with a crocodile. My saurian teacher was a wrestling master and a far better judge than I of my incautious character, the precarious nature of human life, and of various other things I needed to know and have striven to pass onto others.

It is not a minor or inessential feature of our human existence that we are food: juicy, nourishing bodies. Yet, as I looked into the eye of the crocodile, I realised that my planning for this journey upriver had given insufficient attention to this important aspect of human life, to my own vulnerability as an edible, animal being. This was the country of the largest of the living crocodiles, a close relative of the ancient dinosaurs, the Estuarine or Saltwater Crocodile. Not long ago saltwater crocodiles were considered endangered, as virtually all mature animals were shot out of the rivers and lakes of Australia's north by commercial hunting. But after more than a decade of protection, their numbers were beginning to burgeon. The saltwater crocodile is a predator of humans from the distant past, a creature that can move so fast it appears to the human eye as a flash. It was hard for me to judge the size of the one that had attacked and pursued my canoe and now fixed its gaze on mine, for all of it except the head was under the murky water, but it was clear that I aroused intense interest. I now know that an animal that can give its intended prey a misleading impression of its size, can also help them to a less misleading sense of who and what they are.

Of course, in some very remote and abstract way, I knew it happened, knew that humans were animals and were sometimes—very rarely—eaten like other animals. I knew I was food for crocodiles, that my body, like theirs, was made of meat. But then again in some very important way, I did *not* know it, absolutely rejected it. Somehow, the fact of being food for others had not seemed real, not in the way it did now, as I stood in my canoe in the beating rain staring down into the beautiful, gold-flecked eyes of the crocodile. Until that moment, I knew that I was food in the same remote, abstract way that I knew I was animal, was mortal. In the moment of truth, abstract knowledge becomes concrete. You gaze with dumb astonishment as your own death, known only as a shadowy, distant stranger, suddenly rises up right before you in terrifying, technicoloured detail and gasp in disbelief that some powerful creature can ignore your special status and try to eat you.

How had I come to make this terrible mistake about myself, my place, my body? I asked myself, with that sinking sense of serious stupidity that mars many a final moment. Was it a philosophical mistake about identity, the self as disembodied consciousness dissociated from the food-providing self as material body? Or the idea that humans are special, above and apart from other animals? I had no real opportunity to ponder the cultural genesis of my false consciousness, for at that moment the crocodile made its move, leaping from the water so fast I saw only a flash, and grabbing me painfully between the legs before pulling me down into the water. Nor did I pursue the issue later that day as I lay, terribly injured, in the path of the oncoming flood. But I have had many years since in which to think about these disastrous illusions, and to try to track them down.

***

Some events can completely change your life and your work, although sometimes the extent of this change is not evident until much later. They can lead you to see the world in a completely different way, and you can never again see it as you did before. You have been to the limit, and seen the stars change their course. That extreme heightening of consciousness evoked at the point of death is, as many testify, of a most revelatory and life-changing kind—for those who, against all odds, are given a reprieve and survive. The extraordinary visions and insights that appear in those last seconds can be hard to reconcile with our normal view of the world. In the vivid intensity of those last moments, when great, toothed jaws descend upon you, it can HIT YOU LIKE A THUNDERCLAP that you were completely wrong about it all—not only about what your own personal life meant, but about what life and death themselves actually mean.

That's how it was with me, anyway. What is called the 'moment of truth' revealed the world I thought I lived in to be illusory, my own view of it terribly, shockingly mistaken. But the sense of being completely wrong about it all was much more than just being wrong about the value of my own life, and my stupidity in risking it. I don't mean self-castigation or regret, being mistaken about the immense value of your life—the intense perception as you face your end that you've been a fool in risking it, that life is much more precious than you counted it, and that you should have given its preservation much more care. The regret evoked by impending death was there, but there was something else, something much more than regret.

This was a strong sense, at the moment of being grabbed by those powerful jaws, that there was something profoundly and incredibly wrong in what was happening, *some sort of mistaken identity*. My disbelief was not just existential but ethical—this wasn't happening, couldn't be happening. The world was not like that! The creature was breaking the rules, was totally mistaken, utterly wrong to think I could be reduced to food. As a human being, I was so *much more than food*. It was a denial of, an insult to all I was to reduce me to food. Were all the other facets of my being to be sacrificed to this utterly undiscriminating use, was my complex organisation to be destroyed so I could be reassembled as part of this other being? With indignation as well as disbelief, I rejected this event. It was an illusion! It was not only unjust but unreal! *It couldn't be happening.*

After much later reflection, I came to see that there was another way to look at it. There was illusion alright, but it was the other way around. It was the world of 'normal experience' that was the illusion, and the newly disclosed brute world in which I was prey was, in fact, the unsuspected reality, or at least a crucial part of it. But all I saw then was the lack of fit between the experience of being prey and the framework of belief and life I took to be normality. If the framework of normality was true, the lack of fit could only be explained if this experience of being prey was an illusion, was a dream or nightmare. But if it wasn't, I had to face the possibility that the lack of fit was there because both I and the culture that shaped my consciousness were wrong, profoundly wrong—about many things, but especially about human embodiment, animality and the meaning of human life.

Sometimes ordinary experience can trick you, can be profoundly wrong, profoundly out of touch. My most recent encounter with sustained illusion occurred a few years ago on another canoe trip, this time in the far north of Canada. I came to a place on the Peel River where all the landforms I could see around me were strongly marked by parallel strata that tilted slightly upwards. Since the human eye is guided in these circumstances to take the land as its horizontal reference, I experienced a powerful and persistent illusion that we were moving across a level landscape and that the river was running very sharply downhill. But there were some things that didn't fit. The river gradient seemed very steep, but the water was placid and unhurried, without rapids. Our calm movement downriver took on a surreal, dreamlike quality, not at all unpleasant—indeed rather enchanting and liberating, as if we had somehow escaped from normal gravity and entered a parallel universe. It took some reflection on various subtle clues, the little pieces of corrective experience that did not fit, to reveal the presence of illusion and show that it was the river and not the land that was true, on the level.

The illusion revealed by the crocodile encounter was of a different, more philosophical kind, about the meaning of everyday experience. But in the same way it revealed that it was possible for people—as individuals, groups, perhaps whole cultures that subscribe to a particular dominant story—to be completely and systematically wrong about quite simple and basic things—our relationship to food, to one another, the intertwining of life and death, the fleshly, embodied character of human existence—and be quite unaware of it. A few people may come to see the illusion for what it is because they stumble across certain clues, experiences that do not fit the dominant story. Suppose that in the same way as the illusion that the land was on the level, the fact of being always on the 'winning side' of the predation relationship tricks us, conceals from us the real slant of things, the real measure of our animality and embodiment. Now suppose that the clue experiences that can correct the illusion become for some reason increasingly scarce—perhaps because the dominant story itself brings about their elimination! Then the illusion might go on for a very long time, might have to result in real catastrophe, before anyone realises anything is wrong. And by then the culture might be out of touch in a very big way.

That I think is what has happened to Western culture under the influence of the dominant story about our animality. For a modern human being from the first, or over-privileged world, the humbling experience of becoming food for another animal is now utterly foreign, almost unthinkable. And our dominant story, which holds that humans are different from and higher than other creatures, are made out of mind-stuff, has encouraged us to eliminate from our lives any animals that are disagreeable, inconvenient or dangerous to humans. This means, especially, animals that can prey on humans. In the absence of a more rounded form of the predation experience, we come to see predation as something we do to others, the inferior ones, but which is never done to us. We are victors and never victims, experiencing triumph but never tragedy, our true identity as minds, not as bodies. Thereby we intensify and reinforce illusions of superiority and apartness. Since the potential for more corrective and chastening forms of experience has been eliminated from normal life, there is less and less experience available of the type that can correct the illusion.

On reflection, I came eventually to see that I was subject at that moment of truth to an illusion about death and my place as a human being in the scheme of things rather similar to my illusion upon the Peel River. Confronted with the prospect of being food, my sense of who I was profoundly out of whack, in just the same way as my perception of that piece of the Peel River. Then, it seemed as if I had entered a parallel universe in which rivers flow slowly down mountains at the same leisurely pace as they meander across the plain.

I leapt through the eye of the crocodile into what seemed also a *parallel universe*, one with completely different rules to the 'normal universe'. This harsh, unfamiliar territory was the Heraclitean universe where everything flows, where we live the other's death, die the other's life: the universe represented in the food chain. I was suddenly transformed in the parallel universe into the form of a small, edible animal whose death was of no more significance than that of a mouse, and as I saw myself as meat I also saw with an incredible shock that I inhabited a grim, relentless and deplorable world that would make no exceptions for me, no matter how smart I was, because like all living things, I was made of meat, was nutritious food for another being.

Later, because against the odds I survived, I could begin the process of reconciling the two universes. The parallel universe was my very own, this world of experience and embodiment in which I have always lived my life, the world that gave birth to me and has made me what I am. It was because the world in which I was meat diverged so wildly from what I saw as reality that I could not recognise it as the world of my own everyday experience, and had to adopt the 'parallel universe' fiction. But that was a measure of my delusion rather than of its departure from the real world of earthly life. It has been a great struggle for me to recognise and reconcile with this harsh world as my own. That recognition and reconciliation is what this book has to offer.

***

These events provided me with rich material for reflection long after my recovery and left me with many intellectual puzzles around food and death and a strong sense of incompleteness. Why could I not see myself as food—why did it seem so wrong? In what sense was it wrong? Why was being food such a shock? What kind of shock was it? Why did I do such dangerous things and not perceive my danger? Why did I not see myself as subject to these kinds of dangers in this place? Why was I, as a critic of anthropocentrism over many years, able to harbour so many illusions about human apartness? Does this reveal my personal confusion or how deep the sense of human superiority and apartness runs in the dominant culture? Or both? I hope to lay to rest some of these questions here.

For thousands of years, Western religions and philosophies taught that the human was set apart from the animals and the rest of nature, made, unlike them, in the image of God. It was heresy to believe that any species other than humans could be saved or go to heaven, a place of sacredness and perfection reserved exclusively for human beings. God is transcendent, not material, apart from nature, and is for our species alone. Our investment in this special status remains enormous. Despite what we have learnt from Darwin, our culture has been a dismal failure at coming to terms with our inclusion in the animal and natural order, and this is a major factor behind the environmental crisis. It is no trivial matter for a culture which locates human identity outside and in opposition to the earth, in a disembodied universe even beyond materiality itself, to receive the news Darwin brought, of our descent from other animals through evolution.

The Darwinian knowledge has been accepted in some places, after a long struggle, but it has been absorbed at a very superficial, mainly intellectual level.

It has not penetrated into other parts of our consciousness and is still at odds with the deep culture. Most of the dominant culture still resists this knowledge and some is explicitly rejectionist. Even at an intellectual level, there are all sorts of dodges for evading its egalitarian import. For example, Papal doctrine until recently, instructed us that our bodies may have evolved from other animals, but that the real basis of our humanity, our minds have not—they are god-given, and in no way comparable to those of animals. We remain special, as the real owners of the world, the pinnacle of evolution, the ultimate species for whom it was all designed and to whom it all leads.

This way of viewing the world makes it very painful to come to terms with features of conscious animality, insofar as our culture has made of it a painful contradiction—a sidereal identity in a fleshly, decaying body, thinking flesh, knowing flesh, singing flesh, flesh that knows of its own vulnerability. Being food confronts one very starkly with the realities of embodiment, with our inclusion in the animal order as food, as flesh, our kinship with those we eat, with being part of the feast and not just some sort of spectator of it, like a disembodied eye filming somebody else's feast. We are the feast. This is a humbling and very disruptive experience.

Although we may be brimming with fanciful speculation about the place of mind in the world we are still and overriding all, food like all other animals. Our ability to deny this fact and 'stand apart' is dangerously reinforced by our elimination of those to whom we are prey. My answer to this conundrum has been a philosophical one and is positioned within the theory of human/nature dualism.

I see human/nature dualism as a failing of my culture, time and history. Human/nature dualism is a Western-based cultural formation going back thousands of years that sees the essentially human as part of a radically separate order of reason, mind, or consciousness, set apart from the lower order that comprises the body, the animal and the pre-human. Inferior orders of humanity, such as women, slaves and ethnic Others (so-called 'barbarians'), partake of this lower sphere to a greater degree, through their supposedly lesser participation in reason and greater participation in lower 'animal' elements such as embodiment and emotionality. Human/nature dualism conceives the human as not only superior to but as different in kind from the non-human, which as a lower sphere exists as a mere resource for the higher human one. This ideology has been functional for Western culture in enabling it to exploit nature with less constraint, but it also creates dangerous illusions by denying embeddedness in and dependency on nature. This can be seen in our denial of human inclusion in the food web and in our response to the ecological crisis.

Human/nature dualism is a double-sided affair, destroying the bridge between the human and the non-human from both ends, as it were, for just as the essentially human is disembodied, disembedded and discontinuous from the rest of nature, so nature and animals are seen as mindless bodies, excluded from the realms of ethics and culture. Re-envisaging ourselves as ecologically embodied beings akin to, rather than superior to, other animals is a major challenge for Western culture, as is recognising the elements of mind and culture present in animals and the non-human world. The double-sided character of human/nature dualism gives rise to two tasks that must be integrated. These are the tasks of situating human life in ecological terms and situating non-human life in ethical terms.

Although, by definition, all ecologically embodied beings exist as food for some other beings, the human supremacist culture of the West makes a strong effort to deny human ecological embodiment by denying that we humans can be positioned in the food chain in the same way as other animals. Consequently, predators of humans have been execrated and largely eliminated.

**

The eye of the crocodile—the giant estuarine crocodile of northern Australia—is golden flecked, reptilian, beautiful. It has three eyelids. It appraises you coolly it seems, as if seldom impressed, as one who knows your measure. But it can also light up with an unexpectedly intense glint if you manage to engage its interest. This was the mistake I made on that day in February 1985 paddling a canoe on the backwaters.

Since then I have come to understand that the eye of the crocodile, along with the voice of the prey of the crocodile—and one cannot be understood without the other—is also a position to speak from, to think from. It is one I have found illuminating in building a philosophy that can celebrate the world in which we live with joy and understand our current relationship to the biosphere.

But it is a position increasingly shut out, eliminated from the world. To hear this voice requires seeing yourself in ecological terms, in historical–evolutionary terms. This crocodile-eye view is the view of an old eye, an appraising and critical eye that potentially judges the quality of human life and finds it wanting. Crocodiles are the voice of the deep past, covering the time span of the rise and extinction of many species. It is a voice we need to hear but it is increasingly drowned out by loud party music and noisy self-congratulation. Above all, it is drowned out by the sound of humans fighting.

The eye of the crocodile also provides us with a perspective that can help us to see ourselves in ecological terms; help us towards a theory of ourselves in thoroughgoing evolutionary–democratic terms, disrupting our view of ourselves as set apart and special. We need to respond rationally to the environmental crisis by adopting a much more ecologically democratic position. From such a viewpoint we can love fellow humans without needing to maintain an exclusionary stance towards non-humans. To date we have seen ourselves as masters of the universe. In theological times this meant seeing ourselves set apart as the single recipient of divine regard while in modern times we interpret our position as the culmination of the evolutionary endeavour.

Moving from one world to another involves a leap, not because the frameworks of ideas we must leave behind are completely discrete—indeed they may overlap considerably—but because there is a major change in the interpretations of certain keystone concepts so that theories are no longer compatible. Death, like food and being human, is one of those keystone concepts that registers change and sources of resistance to change. Narratives of death and the afterlife give important clues to concepts of ecological identity and membership of an earth community.

In that flash, when my consciousness had to know the bitter certainty of its end, I glimpsed the world for the first time 'from the outside', from outside the narrative of self, where every sentence can start with an 'I'. That story actually entails a process of what Deborah Bird Rose calls 'denarrativisation', whereby Western culture ceased to regard the world as having its own story and started to look at the world as a storyless object. The old, I now know, goes on, although it is no longer a story revolving exclusively around a human subject.

Humour is one way to maintain the 'outside' story. The disruptive and radically humbling potential of the eye of the crocodile perspective has been the basis for several very fine crocodile cartoons which poke fun at the pretences of humanity. One cartoon, by Gary Larsen, shows two large, fat green crocodiles lying on a bank rubbing their tummies appreciatively, while in the stream below floats a broken red canoe, a paddle and a solar topee. One crocodile is saying to the other, 'That was marvellous! No hair, no hooves, no hide, just white, soft and succulent'. Another shows two tourists wearing shorts and tropical gear walking past two concealed crocodiles. One crocodile is saying to the other, 'They look disgusting, but I believe they're very good for you'.

I always found the Larsen cartoon spoke powerfully to me first because I had had a red canoe, and second because I came to feel strongly that I wanted to defend the crocodile's right to eat humans who strayed into their territory. Thirdly, I appreciated how humbling a perspective was that of the crocodile, and one we now stand greatly in need of! The crocodile stands apart from the human and makes a fearless judgement which diminishes human significance. The crocodile is the purveyor of a critical view of humans which cuts us down to size, cuts through our pretensions to be a superior species above the food

17

chain and figures us as just another animal, a particular kind of food, food with pretensions. Yet this important perspective or speaking position is increasingly denied cultural representation and only rarely achieves cult representation.

An understanding of ourselves as food is the subject of horror as well as humour. Horror movies and stories reflect this deep-seated dread of becoming food for other forms of life: horror is the wormy corpse, vampires sucking blood and sci-fi monsters trying to eat humans as in Alien 1 and 2. Horror and outrage usually greet stories of other species eating live or dead humans, and various levels of hysteria are elicited when we are nibbled by leeches, sandflies, and mosquitoes.

But humans *are* food, food for sharks, lions, tigers, bears and crocodiles, food for crows, snakes, vultures, pigs, rats and goannas, and for a huge variety of smaller creatures and micro-organisms. An ecological animalism would acknowledge this and affirm principles emphasising human–animal mutuality, equality and reciprocity in the food web.

All living creatures are food, and also much more than food. In a good human life we must gain our food in such a way as to acknowledge our kinship with those whom we make our food, which does not forget the more than food that every one of us is, and which positions us reciprocally as food for others. A reconceptualisation of ourselves in ecological terms has many aspects, but one of the most fundamental is to begin to think of ourselves in terms of our usefulness to the other elements of our ecosystems, in the same way as other components. One of the most basic ways is to begin to think of ourselves—humbly—as food for others.

Let us then radically revise our conception of food. Being and thinking of ourselves as of use as food for others is the most basic way in which we can re-envisage ourselves in ecological terms and affirm our solidarity with other animals in opposition to the dominant cultural conviction that we humans are set apart, too good to be food. For we are made for the other. Such a mutual use does not mean we exist for them to colonise and destroy as we have colonised and destroyed them. It is simply a re-visioning of our place in more egalitarian terms.

My disbelief about being food, of believing the human to be apart, eaters of others but never ourselves eaten, or that it is profoundly wrong has been the dominant story about human identity, a story of human hyper-separation from nature. This is an old and very powerful story which is in turn linked to our culture's approach to the problem of death.

This denial that we ourselves are food for others is reflected in many aspects of our death and burial practices. The strong coffin, conventionally buried well below the level of soil fauna activity, and the slab over the grave to prevent anything digging us up, keeps the Western human body (at least sufficiently affluent ones) from becoming food for other species. Sanctity is interpreted as guarding ourselves jealously and keeping ourselves apart, refusing even to conceptualise ourselves as edible, and resisting giving something back, even to the worms and the land that nurtured us.

Upon death the human essence is conventionally seen as departing for a disembodied, non-earthly realm, rather than nurturing those earth others who have nurtured us. This concept of human identity positions humans outside and above the food web, not as part of the feast in a chain of reciprocity but as external manipulators and masters separate from it. Death becomes a site for apartness, domination and individual salvation, rather than for sharing and for nurturing a community of life. Being food for other animals shakes our image of human mastery. As eaters of others who can never ourselves be eaten in turn by them or even conceive of ourselves in edible terms, we take, but do not give, justifying this one-way arrangement by the traditional Western view of the human right to use earth others as validated by an order of rational meritocracy in which humans emerge on top. Cannibalism aside, humans are not even to be conceptualised as edible not only by other humans, but by other species.

My proposal is that the food/death imaginary we have lost touch with is a key to re-imagining ourselves ecologically, as members a larger earth community of radical equality, mutual nurturance and support. Our loss of this perspective has meant the loss of humbling but important forms of knowledge, of ourselves and of our world. We can learn to look for comfort and continuity, meaning and hope in the context of the earth community, and work in this key place to displace the hierarchical and exceptionalist cultural framework that so often defeats our efforts to adapt to the planet. This involves re-imagining ourselves through concrete practices of restraint and humility, not just in vague airy–fairy concepts of unity.

Modernist liberal individualism teaches us that we own our lives and bodies: politically as an enterprise we are running and experientially as a drama we are variously narrating, writing, acting and/or reading. As hyper-individuals, we owe nothing to anybody, not to our mothers, let alone to any nebulous earth community. Exceptionalised as both species and individuals, we humans cannot be positioned in the food chain in the same way as other animals. Predation on humans is *monstrous*, exceptionalised and subject to extreme retaliation.

The Western problematic of death—where the essential self is disembodied spirit—poses a false choice of continuity, even eternity, in the realm of the spirit, versus the reductive materialist concept of death as the complete ending of the story of the material, embodied self. Both horns of this dilemma exact a terrible price, alienation from the earth in the first case and the loss of meaning and narrative continuity for self in the second.

Indigenous animist concepts of self and death succeed in breaking this pernicious false choice and suggesting satisfying and ecologically responsive forms of continuity with and through the earth. By understanding life as in circulation, as a gift from a community of ancestors, we can see death as recycling, a flowing on into an ecological and ancestral community of origins. In place of the Western war of life against death whose battleground has been variously the spirit-identified afterlife and the reduced, medicalised material life, the Indigenous imaginary sees death as part of life, partly through narrative, and partly because death is a return to the (highly narrativised) land that nurtures life. Such a vision of death fosters an imaginary of the land as a nourishing terrain, and of death as a nurturing, material continuity with ecological others, especially the lives and landforms of country.

***

Other questions came to my mind later when reflecting on my experience. Why did I do such a dangerous thing and not perceive my danger? Why did I previously not see myself as subject to these kinds of dangers? One way of answering these questions lies in my background in a certain kind of culture, my background relationship to the land I was visiting and the land of home. My relationship, in other words, to place. I was in a place that was not my own and which was very different from my own place. An important part of place is one's sense of the large predators for placing us.

Europe and North America have their wolves and bears, some of which can be a serious danger to the human species. South America and Africa have many species which make walking, camping or adventuring alone in many habitats a dangerous enterprise.

Those like myself who have grown up in the bush of Southern Australia have had our awareness of danger formed in an apparently more benign environment that lacks serious human predators. It is not that danger is lacking in the bushlands of SE Australia. In the forest where I live there are many very dangerous spiders. Snakes, including several that are among the most venomous in the world, are commonly encountered. One of the most important and subtlest dangers is fire.

When I returned home to my current abode in early December last year, the forest was frighteningly dry, there were three bushfires around me and the air was full of smoke. Then a few days later we had one of those wonderful interventions that excite this part of the coast: the Cool Change! Along these coastal ranges over the summer months we experience a great tug of war between two elements, the cool, moist maritime element from the southern oceans versus the hot, dry fire-bearing element, the fire dragon from the scorched heart of the continent. (Of course this good/bad alignment is much too simple—each side has its positives and negatives). In most seasons the moist maritime goddess can be counted on to win, but in drought seasons such as this one the balance is more precarious. Here, every week, the question seems to be: will we make it again this year? Will the silver goddess get here in time to expel the fire dragon? Will we survive?

The southerly change really is Cool. Water trickles steadily into my rain tanks as cool moist cloud sweeps in from the ocean through the forest. I dig out a sweater; lyrebirds are singing again; grasses greening. All the fires around me now seem to be out. The dripping forest feels good now, but I know it's not over yet until we get a lot more rain. It can all change back in a week or two of heat and drying winds into a fire powder keg. You have to be able to look at the bush you love and also imagine it as a smoking, blackened ruin, and somehow come to terms with that vision. I am trying to make my house fire-ready, but in the cool moist airstream of the moment I am finding it hard to sustain the sense of urgency and inevitability that moved my efforts a week or two ago. Now a little hope has returned that I'll be lucky and that the encounter with that particular demon can be yet again postponed. But I know I will have to meet the fire monster face-to-face one day.

Well I'm pleased to report now in mid-January that the silver goddess has won again, that the forest moisture is now very good and the fire element has been expelled—but only for the moment, and only for this local coastal mountain rainforest microclimate. Further west it's still very dry.

Not so in Kakadu which is a very different and much more dangerous environment, one in which I was to learn the agonies of the world from which my safe life in southern Australia had protected me, where the animal fate of being food is extended to the human species.[1]

---

1   This chapter is a revised version of an article published by the journal *Terra Nova* titled 'Being Prey'. It is a vivid blow-by-blow account of the crocodile attack, Val's subsequent rescue and her thoughts about this encounter.

2. Dry season (Yegge) in the stone country

The ripples spread across the turquoise waters of a deep, clear rock-lined pool as I fill a billy with water. Until I shattered their reflections, the peaceful waters mirrored patterns in colour palettes of breathtaking beauty—the green of fringing pandanus and umbilik (*Allosyncarpia*), the unbroken blue of the early dry season skies, and the brilliant orange of the rock face on the pool's opposite edge. I look again at the bright rock face, wondering if the wet season flood of the creek had here exposed the unweathered face of the Arnhem Land escarpment. The top section of the pool consists of shelves of polished, rocky ledges forming a small poolside platform like an intimate stage. The stage is backed by the orange rock face and faces north-west to a group of weathered creek-side rock ledges that rise in ranks like the seats of a Greek theatre. Although the platform looks perfect for a small human dance or dramatic performance, its only present occupants are a small group of human-sized wattles and young eucalypts.

On the lowest part of this platform, on opposite sides of the small fall of water tumbling melodiously into the pool, sit two water monitors. Well named, these large hunting lizards scan the parade of water creatures passing through the channel, always on the lookout for a tasty meal. Every so often one of them dives and returns shortly to its edge position to munch its living feast. Further down the pool, the moist sandy edge spots are covered with delightful crowds of tiny delicate bladderworts like eager debutantes, each pale apricot flower modestly covering its sexual parts with what looks like a white apron with red spots— (very occasionally it has white spots upon red, as if the apron were turned inside out). But the innocent appearance is a trick, for these elegant, shy beauties are in fact carnivorous plants which lure and prey upon the rich insect life of this tropical stream. Predation and food seem pretty big in this environment: even the plants are doing it. In the south, orchids lure insects through their private parts to achieve pollination; here in the north their equivalents, the bladderworts, eat the insects they lure beneath their aprons.

It is hard to imagine anything more innocent and inviting than this superb pool, especially after a long walk with a heavy pack through the midday heat of Yegge, the early dry season in Binitj country of Australia's Northern Territory. But is the innocence of the pool also a trick? What lurks beneath the overhanging banks, in the shadowy caves of roots? I sit for a while, tense and watchful, remembering sharply the grasp of vice-like jaws rising from the water. Here, I try to reassure myself, I am well up into the stone country, where you could encounter at most a freshwater crocodile, the smaller species that rarely inflicts serious damage on humans. You would surely never meet here the fearsome

Saltwater Crocodile, terror of the floodplain and coastal waterways, probably the most dangerous predator for humans on the face of the earth. But doubts still intrude. I have been warned that the Salties, not long ago close to extinction after the ravages of commercial crocodile hunting, seem to be expanding their range in these times of official protection and global warming, moving into the habitat of their smaller neighbours, habitat more or less like this. I'm not taking a chance on a swim just yet.

I resist for now the call of the pool, best to sit and gaze for a while into its green sandy depths. Soon time and place combine to stimulate (or was it insinuate?) some idle speculation about cross-species theatre. What if the natural cycles I see around me were the dramatic subject for which the poolside theatre was the setting, the reverse of our usual order? Might not the drama to be played out there demand both human and non-human actors? Could the plot map the characters onto the struggle between mind and matter, or freedom and justice versus necessity and chaos? How could we express the tensions between perceptions of cruelty and cyclical ways to think about the workings of nature, which correspond roughly to the contrast between the desires of the animal liberationists and ecological perspectives? Perhaps as a conflict between presiding deities, unhappily married—like Jupiter and Juno? Is it inevitable that consciousness is unhappily married to embodiment? If the bladderworts and lizards enact the dramatic struggles of predation lower down the pool, for whom or what might the main upper section of the platform be reserved? What was that shadow I thought I saw among the rocks above the platform, about the right size and shape for a crocodile? Of course, I have to remind myself, I often see these fearsome figures where others see only old stumps, rocks and fallen trees.

At last I take the plunge, swimming at first cautiously, uneasily, then after a while relaxing and letting the green-rayed water soothe my spinifex-punctured limbs. I am still remembering. Lower down, I crossed the sandy floodplain reaches of this very same creek, with some trepidation, on that first journey I made in this country in February 1985. That walk that took me along the western side of this same massif. I then travelled on by boat towards the East Alligator River, that journey which was subsequently so momentous for me, and for others as well, culminating in my narrowly surviving a predation attempt on the river by a saltwater crocodile.

My experience then left me with a huge sense of puzzlement, as if I had somehow stumbled into a sinister unfamiliar world that was not my own, but perhaps the stage-set for a movie like *Jurassic Park*. Now after years of reflecting on those events, and of teaching and writing about the philosophical issues raised by predation, I believe I am at last ready to return and recognise that strange terrifying world as my own. This journey, I hope, will help me to understand the meaning of what happened there not only for my own life, but for life itself, from the perspective of both the eater and the eaten.

The stone country pool invites—then, once you have surrendered to it, seduces and delights. Its freshwater pools of incredible natural beauty and variety offer what must be the world's most irresistible temptations to blissful immersion. But one that is perhaps at the same time the most dangerous. A thriving crocodile population reminds us of the power of Ngalyod the rainbow serpent, who recycles life in this place and performs the integration of land, sky and water. Ngalyod's cycles have made this place a great dialogue between the tropical monsoon elements and the stone country, that great sheet of tilted sandstone that emerges above the Arnhem Land floodplain.

The Rainbow Serpent has made water the key to life in this environment. Here in the immensity of the stone country, where we are probably the only humans for many square miles in a vast and rugged area of protected land, we can safely do without the water purifier I have lugged over many miles of hot spinifex, rock and rainforest. The water is inviting, clear and caressing, its temperature is refreshing, but you can spend luxurious, lazy hours in these pools without getting cold. There is a world of difference between the dialogical encounter and excitement the endless variety of life forms this pool provides and the monological, utilitarian chemical predictability of the suburban pool, dedicated to the sole use of an unhealthy subspecies of the human, harried by time, driving on a mechanical body for empty exercise. The water cycle here is majestic and creative, as the Rainbow Serpent tells, and it is under threat from environmental destruction here as everywhere else.

The Rainbow Serpent's acolytes, the water monitors, yellow diamonds on brown reptile skin, face like an otter, watch me swim by unperturbed, occasionally flicking out a forked tongue in my direction when I come too close. I could have caught one quite easily when I first arrived, could have had it sizzling on the fire for supper. Startled from its watching spot above the falls, it slipped into a submerged but easily reached pothole to hide, one fat leg and part of its tail protruding, an easy catch. But no, the monitors, and everything else here, are stringently protected in the Kakadu World Heritage Area, and anyway, I prefer to enjoy the water monitor in other ways. I will stick to my dehydrated vegetarian package dinner, of whose healthiness I am much less sure. I can imagine the possibility of dining on the juicy water monitor, unlike some modern urban intellectuals, but mine is not a hunting life. I do not universally condemn such a life, which under some conditions has been able to express the condition of the human as a top predator without arrogance and with integrity and honesty. The ethics of eating others is complex and contextual, I believe. But it is the terrible injuries that modern capitalism's interpretation of predation inflicts on its category of economic animals that have made me into a vegetarian, rather than any ascetic distaste for the flesh. Even if the wildlife regulations did not stop me, I have now developed a sensibility of restraint in relation to killing and eating animals which I cannot suspend even for water monitors. They are safe, at least from me.

The pool surface, still when I arrived, is now rippled by water boatmen and by a sharp gust of wind. As if inspired by this arrival, the wattles spring into instantaneous theatrical action. The big gold-tipped wattle tree flowering next to the pandanus waves, rustles and almost sings. The old wattle blossoms she has dropped upon the pool's surface are driven into the far corners of the pool to form a golden brown audience facing the platform. Thus acclaimed, three sinuous young wattle trees dance gracefully on centre stage. The whole performance lasts less than a minute. Action is thought of differently over yonder in the sandstone. From my state of watery relaxation, I take in the scarred, distant body of the massif, eaten away by a thousand million years of hyperactive tropical atmosphere. Here the ancient sandstone plateau is weathered to immense, fantastic ruins that bring to mind enigmatic artefacts from some titanic civilisation of the past. An inchoate sphinx face and a perfect sarcophagus, both the size of battleships, top the towers of the great domed red cliffs that rise to the south.

But tickling and nibbling sensations on my feet and legs bring me quickly back to the immediacy of my own scarred body. Tiny fish are now dining off my skin, gently nibbling, and small, not so gentle freshwater prawns are tugging diligently at the hairs of my big toe. Ow! This tribe of capering crustaceans, or *waagi* as they are called by the Gundjiehmi people who hunt them hereabouts with small wooden spears, are now handing out some distinct nips. The *waagi* are quite willing to eat living flesh. Luckily *waagi* are too small to break the skin directly, but they have other methods. I watch fascinated as one of the larger ones makes for a sore point on my hand, conveys the pieces of scab delicately to its mouth, and then makes a start on the flesh beneath. When I lift my hand from the water it is bleeding. The *waagi* however will only eat you alive if you are foolish enough to act dead. Time to get moving again.

Lower down the pool, near the bladderworts, I encountered the *kunbak*, a small water plant whose fine green fronds represent the hair of the Yawk Yawk sisters. The Yawk Yawks live in the slowly moving water along the edges of this little stream that drains a huge area of the stone country. In the narratives of the Kunwinkju people of western Arnhem Land (part of Kakadu), these sisters are little spirit mermaids with fish tails instead of legs. They dwell in the holes beneath the banks and come out to sing and play where the pandanus grows. From underneath the water they watch women swimming, ever on the lookout for one ready to become their mother, to birth them as human.

Aboriginal people of Arnhem Land use the terms *binitj* for Aboriginal people and *balanda* for settler people. For a *balanda* woman like myself, the Yawk Yawk offer welcome sisterly and binitj travelling company in the landscape, enticing Westerners across the high wall we have tried to build between the human and non-human worlds. We journey, of course, not only with our obvious and immediate human companions but also with an unseen band of cultural company. The Yawk Yawk sisters evoked for me the much loved balanda figure of Alice, also a traveller and a shape-changer, who enriched journeys through the Sydney sandstone landscapes of my own childhood. I wish to join these binitj and balanda sisters in playful company: I too would like to be a shape-changer. I would like to be a wattle.

Many binitj namings invoke narratives like those of the Yawk Yawk. These striking stories function both to impress their meanings cunningly and irresistibly in the memory, and to bind together botanical, experiential, practical and philosophical knowledge, community identity and spiritual practice in a rich and satisfying integration of what we usually place in opposing groups of life and theory. Binitj stories envelope a journey in their land in narrative, so that one travels through a speaking land encountered in dialogical mode, as a communicative partner. By contrast the main *balanda* cultural namings you encounter around here represent a monological relationship to land. Namings like 'Mount Brockman' take no notice at all of this extraordinary place, or of its power and agency. The puzzling, pointless and Eurocentric naming of this great outlier of the escarpment, marked by remarkable and ancient Aboriginal places and rock art galleries, commemorates a European 'discoverer' and finds the place notable only for the accident of its falling in the way of a member of the colonial aristocracy. Such monological namings treat the place itself as a vacuum of mind and meaning, to be filled through the power plays of those in favour with the colonial office or the resource activities of mining companies. This deeply colonised naming practice still disfigures too much of the Australian map, and neither it nor its underlying narrative of eurocentrism and of colonial power is in any way challenged by formal decolonisation exercises like republicanism. It is precisely such cultural practices we have to take on if we Australians are ever truly to belong culturally to this land and develop a mode of exchange that attends to and respects the uniqueness and power of place.

The westering sun finally calls me from the pool. Time to prepare for the evening meal and the avid attentions of those tax collectors of the ecosystem, the mosquitoes. Earlier, when we arrived at this superb pool campsite, it was hot and quiet/hushed, as if everything was resting, even the mountains—all except the murmuring creek and the monitors. Now, as it begins to cool off, new voices come to life. Earth others of this landscape are emerging from cool resting-up places, negotiating and announcing their arrangements for the coming evening.

A sandstone friar bird, noisy and pugnacious, calls a greeting-challenge, and is answered by a second sending back what sounds like a tenfold elaboration on the first, a sassy reply with plenty of brass knobs on (to invoke the term children use to effect escalating insult). A rainbow bird pair, bundles of rainbow colour and ceaseless energy, buzz out the song that accompanies their playful, erotic hunting dance. I briefly envy the wholeness of their existence, apparently a seamless combination of hunting, dancing, singing, eating, and love, thinking of the painful partitions and oppositions we moderns have created in these areas. (When will we understand that smarter is not always better, that greater sophistication and complexity are not always an improvement?). A grey falcon lands in a nearby tree, and the rainbow songs are silenced for the day. Soon the great orange stone sarcophagus on the top of the facing cliff is catching the setting sun, which rests finally on it alone, dying it deep red, the colour of blood.

***

From the poolside camp as our base location, my companion Mark and I set out to walk next day up the creek into the arid interior of this great outlier of the stone country. We journey through a mighty landscape of silent, solemn ruins; the intricate detail of their great wrecked ramparts seems imbued with the heightened significance of dreamscape. Before us, forming the northern walls of our shallow valley, rise battered towers of stone the size and complexity of cathedrals, toppled and leaning at precarious angles, fantastic pieces in some game of giants strewn carelessly across the floor of this rocky world. Every turn of the creek brings new tilted columns, crazy stacks or shady temples into view, new disclosures of the unimaginably infinite variety of the earth narrative that is weathered stone. Each formation is a revelation of wonder to be encountered on its own terms and in its own time, rather than commanded to fit some pre-established schema by a supreme, impatient, all-knowing eye. We are truly in the presence of the old ones.

You do not have to stretch yourself too much here to get a sense of the land as powerful and intentional, ultimately beyond us, one of the old ones, the creator beings. To those of us *balanda*, who have in our conceptual frameworks systematically denied the power of the old ones, experiencing the power of ancestral processes can evoke almost the kind of fear we associate with the eerie. Some mystics believe spirit photography to have the power to reveal the unseen, mysterious shapes and figures that do not appear to the immediate human gaze. Among my snapshots of the place is one unexpectedly showing what appears to be a giant white alien figure standing, one arm extended, in front of what looks like a strange ruined city. Such a sense of power does the background landscape evoke, of being in contact with something much more than you can sense, that this mysterious figure (which I would not presume to call a trick of the light) does not seem at all out of time or place.

But the character of revelation such experience evokes is thoroughly paradoxical, for it is precisely the revelation of the extraordinary character of what the *balanda* framework makes invisible, treats as an utterly familiar and unimportant background—the passage of geological time—that is foregrounded and communicated so powerfully in the eroded grey and red rock ranges that surround us on every side. They confront us sharply with the difficult knowledge of our limitations, for in the complex and intricate narrative that explains the emergence of the correspondingly complex and intricate forms we see around us, we can as human observers never know the full story that matches the intricacy we observe. We can discern only a few of its broader outlines: that all this has evolved through the ancestral processes of sea, rain and wind that have sculpted it through the tides of 1800 million years. To save face, we conveniently dismiss the rest under the rubric of contingency, accident, or formless chaos, belittling all complexities we cannot know or control.

It gets hotter and hotter as we walk up the creek into the higher parts of the stone country. As we leave behind the shady canyons, pools and the creek-side rainforest groves of Allosyncarpia (umbilik), the heat of Yegge is visibly reflected in heat waves rising from a region of much harsher country, great stone expanses where most of the vegetation in sight edges the creek or clings to the sides of distant ranges. The wattles, previously mainly up in the higher and drier parts, have moved down to the creek margins, and sparse spinifex increasingly occupies the broken country that stretches away from the creek. Much of the mobile life in this landscape depends on the small flow of creek water now trickling over and between exposed rocky ledges. The creek itself soon disappears underground into deep fissures, and when we pick it up again gratefully we stop to wet our shirts and hats to keep cool. We are not the only ones here under heat stress. The beautiful grey felty-leaved Gossypium mallow, she of the huge deep pink flowers, has to keep her treasures tightly folded during the heat of the day and dares to open up shop for reproductive business only in the coolness of the late afternoon. It is hard to follow the map, so confusing is the detail of the ruined ranges and so vast the scale of this enigmatic country. Like the vegetation, we cling precariously to the creek, trying to hold ourselves open for the pull of an Aboriginal art site. We have been told there are some galleries here we can visit without offence, but have been given little more than a vague indication of where they might be.

There has been some controversy over the intrusion of *balanda* walkers into this landscape, and talk in some quarters of banning *balanda* bushwalking altogether in Kakadu, although traditional owners are by no means all of that view. Already walking is exceptionally tightly controlled, and all routes and camping sites have to be vetted by the park service. But some suggest that *balanda* walkers are disrespectful and seek to know what had best remain unknown, perhaps to all human eyes to the extent that few binitj now go to these places.

There are many kinds of walking, of course. There is the monological kind of walking that is for exercise only, with no objective of encounter with or knowledge of another beyond the self. (For this type, a Walkman radio is often attached to the head to counter the inevitable boredom). There is instrumental walking, as when you pass rapidly through a place treated as of no interest in itself en route to somewhere else which is your real objective, and experience the others only as places 'along the way', a means of reaching the desired goal. There is also the kind of leisure walking which involves what might be thought of as visual consumption of the landscape experienced as famous, 'must-see' scenery, or collected as an addition to some list of endurance tests, hard-to-reach places you have mastered. (Both of these achievement-oriented types tend to instrumentalise, subordinate or screen out places you encounter along the way other than the designated goal, and treat these with less than respect. Bringing this kind of mind to this kind of place would be very disrespectful.

At the other extreme, there is the kind of walking Thoreau called 'going to the holy land', walking as a dialogical and spiritual practice oriented to meeting and knowing the sacredness of the earth and valuing whatever the journey itself throws up. This can involve a type of journeying (wandering or 'sauntering' in Thoreau's terminology) where you encounter each place along the way with wonder, as perfect, amazing or instructive in itself. In practice, most walking probably involves some more or less conflicting mixture of all of these, and Thoreau's practice of free 'spiritual walking' was more bounded by his time and place than he recognised. But the intense and open kind of experience he describes may have some evolutionary value for the times, not long gone, when our human survival depended on the quality of our knowledge of the land.

We may be programmed by our evolutionary inheritance with the neural capacity to register the land by walking through it, for a landscape you have travelled through on foot can stay fresh in the memory for an extraordinary length of time, and can live in your dreams, sometimes for decades. Thoreau's successors' idea of sacred wilderness as pure nature and of 'human interference' as inevitably degrading the land is not very convincing in this country, where the presence of great galleries of rock art testifying to human habitation over a period of 20,000 years adds immeasurably to its richness, power and fascination. Although we may have our doubts about the applicability here of concepts of wilderness, the wilderness movement has helped to foster several dialogical approaches of great value in an increasingly over-rationalised and monological world. One of these is the wandering, crossroad mind, which can accept as its muse the contingency of the journey, valuing the unplanned, the unintended as contributions to a dialogical exchange with the world, as sources of wisdom and revelation.

Wilderness tends to be understood, however, as something that is separate from land that is used, land that supports us. There is a sundering, a splitting in this outlook that differs from an Indigenous understanding of unity of place. For the people who live here wilderness (wildness) was not a special place set apart as sacred in contrast to the profane earth. For them all the earth was sacred and there was no necessary split between use and respect.

Another aspect of this outlook is the understanding of the importance of embodiment. The intense, intimate and physical bond of knowledge with the earth to be gained by walking opens up a form of conversation with the earth's great body which can only be entered into through the answering effort of our own human bodies. Wilderness travellers must carry survival on their backs and measure themselves as limited and only half-hardy animals. Through such a journey you come to encounter nature in many forms and in the active rather than the passive voice, and to know the land in the mode of a lover, as a wonderfully elaborated, beloved and communicating body.

In the dualistically gendered Western story of spirituality in which the male is identified with an interior and ascetic 'perennial' spirituality that turns away from the body and the material world, and the female with the 'immanent', material, and mundane concerns opposed to spirituality so interpreted, many things that may be important for our survival cannot be expressed. Among these is the possibility of a materialist spirituality that explores and rejoices in the body of the world, knowing it as thoroughly and physically as you can know the body of a lover. In this direction may lie the possibility of a spirituality that is not etherealised or other-worldly, that fully celebrates the nourishing capacities of the earth and knows the sacredness of the everyday, the here and now, of the mundane or quotidian.

If walking provides an opportunity to encounter the power that is in the land, to experience it in terms of a dialogical rather than monological relationship, it can also provide a spiritual encounter at various levels with the narratives of time written in the land. The work culture of late capitalism casts time as the enemy of profit, its elixir of eternal life. This distorted framework has deprived us of much. In it time plays a largely instrumental role as the medium in which certain goals are to be achieved or projects completed. Time is an enemy, an oppressor, a hard and painful taskmaster who will destroy us in the end. An intense and intimate foot journey through the stone country generates a powerful and different experience of time—as geological time actively shaping the extraordinary sandstone ruins, as evolutionary time creating the animal life around us, as the human time evinced in the rock art galleries, and as personal 'time out of time', time to draw with a finger in the sand, time to envy the rainbow birds, time to reflect on and integrate experience. Here in this place, under these conditions, time becomes a teacher and travelling companion, a friend who will carry us away. Time is not the medium, time is also the message.

The day progresses, getting hotter. Almost as we are ready to turn back, we reach a point where from the creek bed we see a long low line of collapsed rock that suggests the outline of a cave. The etiquette is to call to make contact, establish our presence, ask permission to approach. My own ringing cooee call is well practised, since I spent much of the previous summer walking in grizzly bear country in the northern Rockies, where you must call constantly to warn the grizzlies of your presence and avoid disconcerting and dangerous surprises. ('That silly Cooee call again! Another loud-mouthed, tasteless Australian, dear,' one can imagine them yawning).

'Cooee!' I call out loudly. Back from the rock face comes the cooee call, just as loud and astonishingly clear. 'It's Val and Mark, can we come up?' 'Come up!'—comes the response, strong and unhesitating. Binitj perform this calling ceremony to let the ancestors know they are present and to seek their permission to enter. What could be the point of such a practice of seeking permission for *balanda*? I answer: to acknowledge power in the land, to respect and acknowledge the place as agent and as presence or presences, whatever these may be; and to express a dialogical understanding of relationship to the earth as communicative partner. Also to register respect for Aboriginal culture, its creations and customs, and for any artefacts that might be present. And to be open to and respectful of Aboriginal narratives of landscape.

The cave is cool and dim, and the magnificent art gallery on the cave walls well-guarded by ranks of great stone blocks fallen from the roof. Upon the walls of the ochre-whitened passages running beneath the shattered roof we recognise figures associated with several prominent themes in Binitj culture—the double rainbow serpent entwines itself, recycling turtles and fish, kangaroos and humans, rain and creek water. We admire the powerful realisation, close observation of the paintings, wondering at their meaning. Then, round the corner, we gasp and clutch each other. Upon the wall, outlined clearly in red ochre, is the almost life-sized profile of an animal that has been extinct upon mainland Australia for perhaps 5,000 years, the Thylacine or marsupial wolf. There is no possible doubt about the subject of the painting: the stripes depicted across the rear of the body are diagnostic along with the body shape and bearing.

The person who executed this painting was familiar with the thylacine. The animal in this painting bears its extraordinary tail aloft not as an afterthought or optional extra, like a dog, but as a powerful and crucial continuation of its body.

Then we see something else. Directly underneath the painting lie a set of large, white doglike droppings looking only a week or two old. Perhaps these are those of the thylacine's canine rival, the dingo, or perhaps, as I am not unwilling to think, they have been left by a spirit Thylacine itself. We are again in the presence of the old ones, the ancestors.

***

Leaving at last and reluctantly the cave and its coolness, its encounter with time, we enter another remarkable and richly symbolic realm of old ones beyond it, a whole Valley of Balanced Rocks. These figures of eroded stone, representing the oldest and most resistant pieces of the sandstone sheet still somehow against all odds bravely carrying their form into the present, often take a visual form that eerily recalls a shrouded animal or human head. Above the cave gallery they are planted on the skyline on each side of the valley. Always we are in the presence of the old ones, but nowhere more clearly than among such highly weathered rocks. Weathered rocks are among the oldest children of the earth and its surrounding aura of atmosphere. They are, according to the earliest accounts, the product of the marriage struggle between mother earth and father sky. The balanced rock represents the maximum in resistance to the processes of destruction, the original sandstone sheet distilled down to the smallest possible unit of survival, and one not likely to survive for very much longer, one already struggling in the river of time.

This form of the balanced rock has great personal meaning for me. It was a form I attached great significance to in my youth in the Sydney sandstone. Although this is a much younger and less exposed body of stone, the balanced rock is a form created with some regularity by the weathering of sandstone. Balanced rocks were for me symbols of presence, symbols of balance, but also symbols of life's danger, of vulnerability that cut close to the bone: we can fall, we are balanced, our lives are kept open precariously. It is curious that these old wise rocks should so often take a form that recalls a shrouded animal or human head, This form is the sandstone's warning to all embodied individual life: It says, I am about to decompose and crumble, losing my individuality and organisation, but in the process creating others. In the same cause you, you living ones, must die, and since life is defined by its attempt to resist the inevitable decomposition, loss of form, you will finally have to surrender to something you do not want, that which of all things you do not want, to death.

It is curious on another count that these oldest, most tested rocks should so often take a form that recalls a shrouded human or animal head, for that would seem to place them alternatively as symbols of consciousness or meaning— which some identify—too narrowly I think—with humanity. In Cartesian and neo-Cartesian ideology this would be a paradoxical symbolism, since across the great Cartesian divide the non-conscious have nothing in common with the conscious and could not represent them. The balanced rock is therefore a counter-Cartesian symbol, representing the world's resistance to hierarchical Cartesian orderings. It represents also certain aspects that are common in our animal condition, questions of vulnerability and security of life tenure that really mark the difference between the realms we call nature and those we call culture. Animal liberationists tend to assume a domestic and tenured life. The balanced rock is for me a symbol of predation, of the cyclical aspects of nature.

But the balanced rock has meaning of this kind for another reason also, for it was the symbol I saw also on that fateful day, just before my encounter with the crocodile, that caused me to turn and come back when I did, just in time to meet what was waiting for me.

***

We returned to the coolness of the pool for the evening, to rest and to prepare for our departure the following morning. Finally, as we are about to leave we are granted a further layer of revelation. I discover the paintings of the rainbow serpent on the orange cliff behind the platform on the pool. I see at last why the cliff glows so brilliantly.

The old one shines with power and presence that encompasses and nullifies the binaries with which I have been wrestling.

3. The wisdom of the balanced rock: The parallel universe and the prey perspective

I leapt through the eye of the crocodile into what I have now come to think of as a *parallel universe*, one with completely different rules—the Heraclitean universe where everything flows—where we live the other's death, die the other's life. This is the universe represented in the food chain whose logic confounds our sense of justice because it presents a completely different sense of generosity. It is pervaded and organised by a generosity that takes a Heraclitean perspective, one in which our bodies flow with the food chain. They do not belong to us; rather they belong to all. A different kind of justice rules the food chain, one of sharing what has been provided by energy and matter and passing it on in what Gary Snyder refers to as, 'the sacramental energy-exchange, evolutionary mutual-sharing aspect of life—that sharing of energies, passing it back and forth, which is done by literally eating each other'.

But in the individual justice universe the individual subject's universe is like the person-as-the-walled-moated-castle-town. It is under constant siege and desperately, obsessively seeking to keep the body—this body made out of food—away from others and retain it for ourselves alone. Of course we know the walled-moated castle will fall in the end but we try to hold off the siege as long as possible while seeking always more and better siege-resisting technology that will enable us to remain self-enclosed.

In the individual/justice universe you own the energy volume of your body absolutely and spend much of that energy defending it frantically against all comers. Any attempt by others at sharing is regarded as an outrage, an injustice, that must be resisted to the hilt (consider our reaction to the overfamiliar gate-crashers at our high-class feast—mosquitoes, leeches, ticks. These outrage our proprietary sensibilities). In the other, Heraclitean universe, being in your body is more like having a volume out from the library, a volume subject to more or less instant recall by other borrowers—who rewrite the whole story when they get it.

There is no corridor that links these two universes. They are two radically different systems—incommensurable ways of conceiving the world. There is no nice, sedate orderly way of getting out of the individual justice world into the food-chain world. No, you have to leap, wildly and desperately, to get into the Heraclitean universe—and what I leapt through was a golden hoop, the eye of the crocodile.

The eye of the crocodile showed me that there really is a world in which we are all food. As the crocodile pulled me out of my normal universe and down into that watery parallel universe I thought that the world revealed there was one of terrible injustice, indifference and grim necessity. I now think differently. Now I have thought about it more. I think the food chain world is a world of radical and startling equality—it is not unfair, it treats all the same way.

According to Eskimo shamans the greatest danger we face in life is that our food consists of souls. The dilemma we face is seeing the other as food and as souls both at the same time. That is the trick—the wisdom of the balanced rock. We have to see from both these worlds. The wisdom of the balanced rock tells us as humans we live and have our home in both these worlds, although we do not know we do.

Oh, we know about it intellectually, some of us, who've learnt about ecology but experientially we don't know it. Or we only know it experientially exclusively from one position in it—from on top, the perspective of the predator. Some of us have even lost contact with that and think our food comes from the shops where we buy it. This predator perspective gives us a distorted view. It prevents us from thinking in terms of an exchange, a radically levelling exchange.

Instead, from that only-predator angle we come to think the food chain reflects our species' greater worth and we try to remake everything so that it reflects that outlook back to us. This is how we confirm to ourselves the idea that it's our role in life as humans to always have the upper hand. It enables us to justify decimating crocodile populations when any of them have the gall to puncture our illusion. The top–down angle of seeing the food chain always from above is corrupting and distorting. In fact, we don't really know it at all, not as other creatures know it.

We don't ever know its terrible logic fully, experientially, until we have to give our bodies up—in my case a good quality body in perfect working order—give them up to some other life form. When we know the Heraclitean universe fully as the prey knows it, then we know ourselves to be human in an astounding and utterly dismaying way. We suddenly know about giving up that precious, inviolate body—to the jaws of the crocodile! Another borrower recalls the volume—and we haven't even finished reading/writing it!

So who was I to deny the crocodile the food of my body? In the logic of the Heraclitean universe the food of my body, representing the body as energy–matter, never belonged to me. It always belonged to the ecosystem. Its belonging to me is a fundamental illusion in the Heraclitean universe—an illusion that is imported from the other universe. And it was this illusion from the individual justice universe I had just been grabbed out of that underlay my disbelief and outrage.

If the 'meat' we are does not belong to us then the predator is neither a master nor a monster. We have to see things from both universes. This is the wisdom of the balanced rock. The prey perspective can help us see the absurdity and arrogance and parochialism of our assumption that we can impose our moated castle-person claims, in any general way, on the ecological universe. If, thinking solely in the terms of the person-justice universe, we believe that meat is misery we will indeed soon persuade ourselves to leave the 'world of changes' behind us and return to the comfort of the old themes of transcendence, somatophobia, and alienation.

The boundary and radical difference between what I am calling the person/justice and the food/ecological framework is real. I have been there, I have journeyed to this other world in which we are all food, and I have come back, like the one who journeyed out from Plato's Cave, to tell you that it is real. There is an incommensurability which shuts these two worlds off from each other. They exist as parallel universes, in different dimensions. Yet, we exist in both simultaneously. They do not invalidate one another, except when people mistakenly try to reduce one to the other or make other mistakes resulting from human arrogance. These lead us to divide the world between the one in which you are a person-subject from an individual justice perspective, and that other, older shocking, subversive and denied world in which you are food.

I received many letters from religious folks when I was recuperating in hospital who wrote saying they believed I had been saved for a purpose. For a long time I discounted such views but now I think perhaps the task those events have given me is becoming clearer, although I would not concede the teleology of my individual salvation. My task is to remind people of the wisdom of the balanced rock. It is to show people how each universe exists and how each limits the other. It is to discover their relationship and how we can move conceptually between the justice and ecological frameworks. This, of course is the great conflict between animal justice and ecology perspectives which has vexed so many environmental philosophers.

We have to learn to see from both worlds, for we live in both. We will be seriously astray if we fail to realise that both are our home. Unreserved affirmation of predation requires, as it were, blotting out one of these worlds. To argue that being eaten is bad for the prey animal but valuable for the predator, that the violent death of the hunted gives life to the hunter and should be regarded not as value lost but rather as 'value capture', fails to open up the boundary between the two worlds. Taken to its extreme, unreserved affirmation of predation requires what is an even more problematic illusory assumption, the standard one that humans exist in the world of culture and animals are in the other 'food' world of nature. This is the ultimate human supremacist illusion. The reality is we are both of us in both worlds at once.

The realisation that you are eating misery is only possible from one of these worlds. From the other the very thought is unthinkable. Misery in the Heraclitean world is a meaningless concept. To argue from the point of view of misery alone is to clearly deny the ecological framework in which we are all food. This is to deny our own availability in practice while insisting on that of animals. We must either recognise our own availability or insist on the non-availability of other animals. To do otherwise is to covertly appeal to the dualism of the humans-in-justice/animals-in-nature framework.

It is also false to see the boundary between these universes as coinciding with the wild /domestic boundary. Living within an urban and domestic/cultivated sphere does not preclude being in an ecosystem framework. Likewise, the wild can be subject to the perspective of individual justice in various ways. Staring into the eyes of the crocodile the predator/prey conversation I had with myself was precisely about the boundary and transition between these worlds.

These two worlds qualify each other and an unqualified affirmation of predation requires looking at it from only one side. Affirmation requires we confront the reality of both. Although they are parallel, they are not completely independent. Completeness requires a recognition of both along with an understanding of why and how they differ. Being prey helps here as you have to confront the reality of both. A truly embodied knowledge of the self is not possible until you have experienced both worlds and realised embeddedness in both. Somehow, we have to live in both worlds and find viable ways to cross between them.

I have given an experiential picture of these two parallel universes as starkly different because I wanted to honour and reflect my own experience of their shocking, radical otherness. The question remains whether this difference between the part of the universe we can control and the part we will never control is ineradicable. On the one hand, they can be regarded as being as incommensurable as the levels of description involved in physics and morality. For example we might take the difference between talking about a person as the physicist might see them and talking about the same person as a friend, wife or husband might see them. Perhaps we can simply allow this difference to coexist, regarding the two kinds of knowledge as irreducibly different. From this point of view they do not have to compete or contest with one another about who is really real and it would in fact be a fundamental mistake to reduce one to the other. We must, in acknowledging this difference, aim to react to each as is appropriate for it so that we do not allow ourselves to be turned into a sore, bleeding wound or a monster of indifference by bringing to each sphere the reactions appropriate to the other.

On the other hand however, it seems imperative that we try to smooth out the edges between the two universes. To do so acknowledges the tension between them and acknowledges us as beings who live in both worlds. To acknowledge the soul of our food is to acknowledge that both we ourselves and what we eat belong to both worlds; it is to try to bring these worlds into harmony at the point where they touch. This is also the point where what we eat morally touches our lives. It is the point at which we have to do right by our food and acknowledge its generosity. It calls on us to be generous in our turn and relinquish the desire for a mean-spirited self-maximisation that takes as much from each life we use as we possibly can. It requires we learn to be generous with ourselves and generous to all other life by honouring those always animate others whose generosity provides our food and ultimately takes us as food in our turn.

Is there any justification for keeping nature and culture apart in mutual purity? Emphatically no. In opposition to the human desire to succour nature and adhere to the old story of nature as red in tooth and claw, an uncaring sphere of injustice, I advocate the need to make up for your own and others' callousness. To confine criticisms of pointless suffering to the realm of culture yet to see suffering as a necessary aspect of natural selection, as an essential aspect of the survival of the species is to argue that a similar ethic of compassion is not appropriate in nature and the two forms of pain in these different spheres are not analogous. It is to see us as no longer buffeted by natural selection in the same way as those species who live in the wild.

However, although misery and pain within the animal/food world cannot be viewed in just the same way as it is from within the human/justice world, our experience of the human/justice world gives us a sense of solidarity with the striving of all creatures, and this sense of solidarity is as valid a perspective as the necessity-of-suffering perspective that emanates from the animal/food world. I am vividly reminded of moments when, for example, I find myself urgently backing up my car after spotting a helpless and terrified parrot hit, lying in the middle of the road but obviously still lively, still with a chance. Quick, I think, before the next car comes by! (Once, to my grief, disgust and resignation I saw a road tortoise squashed flat in the time it took me to stop the car and run back to rescue it). I pile out of the car, race furiously up the road to where the parrot lies. I spot the mate waiting anxiously and fearfully in the nearby tree, poised for flight. The stricken one must have just been hit—quick now, I can hear another car approaching around the bend—just time to reach out and grab the small pulsing red body, despite my fear of her tearing bite. But she lies passive in my hand and I reach the cover at the side of the road and lift her into a nice thick bush, feel her wriggle free. I know she will be OK and with a sense of gladness for her small life, so red and joyful, I return to my car. Watch out, I say to myself, which universe is this? But do you really need to know? If it needs to it will define itself.

Incommensurability was indeed my experience when I accidentally fell, like Alice in her tumble down the rabbit hole, through the connecting tunnel of the crocodile, from the one system into the other. So utterly strange to one another did they seem and so utterly astonished was I by their supposed incongruence that the challenge now is not that of studying up but of studying down. It is actually the reasons why our culture has supposed them to be so remarkably incongruent, presented them as incongruous, that I must try to study.

As a child in the grim, toyless days of World War II, I spent many happy hours engrossed in an old Wonder Book. Its frayed red cover embossed with a trumpeting African elephant, the wonder book was a childhood cornucopia which spilled from its tattered black-and-white pages the marvellously varied and amazing creatures of the planet. This was a pre-war edition, innocent of the idea of extinction, except for skeletal dinosaurs. The book presented a Eurocentric view of the forest world, its Indigenous peoples and its animals, affirming their supposedly primitive vitality. But the half-conquered world it showed me still seemed wide and bountiful, clothed with the deep, lush forests where most of these marvellous beings made their homes. To the European imagination, the forest world it showed was inexhaustibly virgin and still largely unexplored, beckoning the imagination as a place of mystery, danger, surprise, and self-dwarfing age and grandeur. Wonder, and anticipation of a world of marvels that would one day be yours, were what the old book evoked.

The real world that I found outside my windows was rich enough to confirm in immediate, daily experience the old book's promise of adventure and revelation in the enchanted forest. Majestic Sydney Blue Gums and smooth, salmon-trunked Angophoras surrounded the clearing made on the sandstone for our little mixed farm, which was plucked free of trees by my father's sweat just as the chickens we raised and sold on our little roadside stall were plucked free of feathers by my mother's night-time labours. My mother's weary work left me an unusual degree of freedom to enter the beckoning forest. I became a forest wanderer almost as soon as I could walk, venturing far enough unreproved to gain familiarity with the forest fringing our clearing and some of its more arresting inhabitants. These included snakes, goannas, and a rich variety of ferocious bull-ants.

I was tutored at home and formally registered, like so many bush children of the time, in Correspondence School. But the bush was my real school. It supplied most of my friends, adventures and conversations, often inspired by those of my favourite fictional character, the fearless and philosophical Alice. My wonderland included delightful, sandy wildflower country interspersed with bold, mysterious rock formations which I could explore at will, with no one to ridicule or restrain excesses of conversational familiarity with the other inhabitants. My mother's striking common names for the flowers—Grandfather's

Whiskers, Spiderflower, Bottlebrush, Belrose—were supplanted later by colder scientific terms whose abstract distance could never break that bond of our early familiarity.

But there was a worm in my apple, a fault in my Eden. It was the fault of devaluation of what is around you, of the everyday, the substance of life, in favour of a distant abstract ideal or heaven which leaves everything drained of light, life and beauty. It makes the colours duller and destroys one's receptivity to beauty. Australia with its cultural cringe has, like other settler colonies suffered badly from this syndrome. Despite the wildflower glory, I puzzled about whether the landscape I experienced daily conformed to proper ideals of beauty. It didn't look at all like the pictures my aunties had on their walls, the idealised mountains, parks and formal gardens of the distant place that I still heard spoken of as 'home'. Australians of those times complained often about the endless grey bush and its inexhaustible dullness and monotony, still often looking to a half-remembered Europe for visions of beauty. My third generation parents had gone part-way towards breaking with these colonial values, and I was taught to enjoy and admire the bush, and not to pick the wildflowers or harm the creatures. Yet some unconscious baggage from my cultural milieu remained an obstacle to full and public affirmation of my surroundings.

Yet mostly the sensuous richness of the forest world around me was an overwhelming joy, immediate and undeniable, that won out against this thief of the moment's joy. In summer the forest unfolded its ecstasy of creamy, honey-scented myrtle blossom, dwarf apple, bloodwood and Kunzea, to delight the nose and drive the beetles wild. The nectar-filled Banksia candles were there for the honeyeaters each autumn, burning orange brilliant as the sun foretold winter sunsets. From August onwards, white Tick Bush, pink Boronias and Waxflowers, red Grevilleas and the well-timed Christmas Bells were a feast for the eye, each with its retinue of birds and insects thirsting for a piece of the action. This was a reproduction-centred world, the work it seemed, of an imagination of great fertility entirely uninhibited by any taboos about cross-species sex.

Like Alice who goes sailing, dreaming among the rushes, among the pink, white and blue waterlilies which she picks, I lived a little girl's dream of a world where even the stones might speak, where animals and plants spoke and were all active forces in life. This world was a lover. Nature was full of presences, presences such as the lyre bird, a bird lover calling through the forest, with his rivals calling up the powers of the forest. And so somehow during these childhood wanderings I learnt to think of the world like this, as a lover, and I acquired an unquenchable thirst for life, for the wisdom of the land. An enriching perspective but perhaps incautious. Perhaps this background explains in part why I met the crocodile like a child who has just become aware of the evil in the world, a sharply demonic experience of some great wrong done to another.

In earlier puritan times, nature was pushed away and seen as an evil animal realm in which civilised rules and practices were abandoned in favour of wholesale licence. Nature from this perspective was the wild, threatening female other who must be brought under control and harnessed in the garden. The garden was depicted, by this suspicious, civilising and crusading culture, as the realm of collaborators and domesticated things around the house. It existed in opposition to the realm of the wild.

This is an outlook that decides that, rather than deal with the dangerous things out there that could cause you a moment's inconvenience or even something as terrifying as a mosquito bite, it is preferable to stay within the comfort zone and forget about the rest. The result is that we are now faced with answering the question of what our relationship with the wild must be. Can there really be such a thing as the old regime, the old order of the world with its evolutionary time? Surely there is a real point in solidarity with that world, that vivid world of sharp colours, of quickening pulse, that comes into focus again when you know that the next moments and your decisions in those next few moments will decide your life or death. That is something that sends you spinning through the tunnel at a frightening speed to arrive with a very big bump, a terrible bump, in the parallel universe. For in the death moment we are reclaimed once again by the sphere of nature, of death as nature, and especially so when we die by a predator of nature—as do the other beings we have said are not of our sphere. But we can only comprehend all this through our cultural understandings. Culture, therefore, has a very big and responsible role to play.

First, we should certainly stop expecting an old man with a white beard to hold our hand and guarantee us a world where we all get just what we deserve. Equally we need to stop telling elaborate and patently ridiculous stories about the problem of evil and how it was sent to test us and save the day, or take us away into a better world somewhere else that will look after us and soothe our every want and which will make up for all the injustices of this one. These ideas bear no resemblance to the actual ecological world we live in. It is time we faced up to the fact that we're here and we must try to tell a story that brings the two worlds into some greater congruence and balance.

What sort of story would we have to tell to create a crocodile narrative as a narrative of justice? That is the key question—what sort of story would you have to tell to bring the two worlds together? To be able to see into each from the other one, not to experience that alarming doubleness of the duck-rabbit— now we can see this way, but not that. Rather than a sort of blindness we need to develop a double vision.

The need to explain my own lack of consciousness of the two worlds led me to re-examine the denial of materiality or corporeality in Western culture. My reaction to the crocodile showed me I was not fully liberated from the influence of the ideology common to white Western inhabitants of 'culture'. Although humankind is known to have evolved from the same genetic stock as all other primates and to be closely related to all living things we endlessly engage in activities and beliefs that seem to minimise our connections to other animals. My dramatic entry into the Heraclitean universe opened my eyes and made me acutely aware that we are not in fact different from other animals but material beings vulnerable to death and decay. By keeping ourselves separate from, and ignorant of, this other universe, we maintain a distinction that provides protection from deeply rooted anxieties about mortality and our supposedly superior human status. By imagining that we live solely within culture we can allow ourselves to think that our lives count more than the lives of other physical beings. At base, it is our bodies that we find a particular problem because, unlike our minds, they remind us of our animal limitations.

So what sort of story would enable us to connect the two universes, to interweave them at the level of personal and immediate life as well as social life? It seems to me that the ingrained mind/body dualism in Western culture prevents us from knowing the story of our ecological embeddedness in any way except as it were distantly and at some great remove, in the abstract manner of narrative science or in the same kind of way I discover facts about the state of outer space or Uranus. Normally it seems as if our culture is so constructed that we live in one of these worlds and just know about the other via this removed, abstract kind of knowledge or through an occasional visit to the summer wonderland aspect of nature.

In other words, we live our lives in a human-made world of culture and we define ourselves in terms of human justice. We forget that our lives of culture grew out of the older world that has somehow now floated clear from it—or so it thinks—except that occasionally there are line breaks, interruptions to transmissions, and recently some of the system alarms have been going off at regular intervals. But we have long ago stopped paying much attention to the dials that tell us what is going on in the 'other' system because we are engaged in a competitive game played among a large human population, a scramble for survival in a gigantic machine that runs on the rationality of maximising and concentrating property formation.

So we are not looking in that direction, although occasionally another breakdown forces itself on our attention and causes us to cast a glance back at the dials. It is especially at the point of death and food that the two systems converge on a personal level. So there is an obvious need for a guiding narrative, or better, a set of narratives which reposition us personally in nature. These must also operate at the economic level. They cannot be simply stories of 'visiting' the other domain, of being a summer good-time girl holidaying briefly in nature before returning to the 'proper' sphere of culture.

We are in desperate need of stories that create much greater transparency of these relationships in our day-to-day lives. We must once again become a culture of stories—stories that link our lives with the Great Life which some call Gaia, but all should call by names of their own devising. This is the real meaning of ecological literacy, to have stories that speak of the culture/nature boundary and of where the two cultures meet. Instead we have one discourse about the domain of culture (us) and another discourse, formulated in an especially detached and distant way, about the domain of nature (them). Our conviction that 'we' live in culture and 'they' live in nature is so strong that all that is left is a passionate story about consciousness, history and freedom—about us—and another story about fiercely uninvolved causation and clockwork—a story about them.

The dualistic Christian/Western framework of alienation and material denial has erased our connecting narratives at a number of key meeting points. I am here concerned specifically with those of food and death but there are others that also create dead areas or voids, places of insensitivity where we have no contact structures and no useful guiding stories.

The Western dualistic construction which proclaims separate and never meeting realms continues to hinder these crucial constructions and connections. It allows us to deny grief and mourning for the suffering that animals such as wombats endure in severe drought conditions. I cannot ignore the grief I feel for animals that I have picked up injured or dying—the glimpse of their perfection and the knowledge that they are dying—the robin thrown onto the ground at my feet whose yellow and grey perfection I could only gasp at with grief and contrition as it died slowly in my cupped hands. Or there was the fairy penguin I found washed ashore on a Tasmanian beach, dead from starvation due to waves of disease spread throughout the local pilchard population (a main food source for fairy penguins) by foreign pilchards imported to provide food for farmed salmon. We know that such animals are individuals who often value and know themselves as such and it is important that we should do the same.

The polarity between nature and culture is of the type Marilyn Frye discusses in terms of the feminist project. She argues that it is necessary to move beyond a concept of woman as 'deficient male' to the idea of woman as 'positively-other-than'. What is at stake here is whether current, environmental categories are interpreted as inclusive instead of overlapping.

We cannot ignore the fact that all our food is souls. In my opinion, it is misguided to follow the example of vegetarian imperialists who aim to eliminate any ensouled food by insisting that only non-ensouled food can be eaten. This placing of ourselves outside the food chain and the exchange of reciprocity in food and death and then trying to impose this on other cultures is a dangerous denial. Such alienated vegetarianism has a direct relationship with the dualism of Descartes and the Cartesian separation of moral orders. It equates culture with consciousness and nature with clockwork mechanisms devoid of feeling and governed solely by instinct.

It is this attitude that allows us to treat our food so badly. The factory farmed animal has already been desouled in advance and constructed as future food. The animal becomes just the living end of the production line; it's just meat, mere denigrated, lowly matter. We cannot admit we are eating souls. How can our food be sacred in the way described by Gary Snyder at the start of this chapter if we view ourselves and it through these lenses? I believe vegetarianism in this alienated form is also the product of this mindset.

Despite the main message of ecology that we live in both worlds there remains a great deal of conflict around these issues among environmentalists. I believe this is because we have eliminated the stories that connect the two realms due to our alienated conceptions of the key events in human life where the culture/ nature stories come together.

What is holding us up from resisting this piece of imperialism is the insistence on not construing the ecological sphere as a sphere of justice. We need to employ a richer understanding of ethics that gives an important place to emotionality and particularity. Jim Cheney has indicated ways in which this might be developed by arguing for stories in which the use of metaphor is an apt vehicle for introducing new conceptions of theory and the self, or knowledge and the knower. Justice in the ecological sphere has tough rules that we have shown great resistance to accepting. It consists of a very radical egalitarian framework in which you have your little piece of life force for just so long as it's not wanted by another. These are the Heraclitean rules where your body does not belong to you. There is no delineation of an individual justice framework. However, from the standpoint of a human justice system that doesn't mean we must ourselves treat the whole thing, the more-than-human world in the same way. We are not solely nature and quite a lot of localised parts of 'nature' work in accordance with a sense of individual value. It is a fallacy to assume that we cannot mix realms. What is crucial is to do so in non-appropriative ways. It is possible to make different rules that we will care about and consider individuals where it is appropriate.

We know for example, that crocodiles value individuals in ways that are similar to our own story. There is no reason why we cannot adopt their own standards as a mark of respect for this localised community and for the larger system that allows it to thrive. The alienated vegetarian, I believe, does not admit more than one standard and construes the animal predator as simply outside ethics rather than an operator in a different ethical framework. To see the predator as outside ethics requires positioning them as ethical non-actors—like a child or disadvantaged human categories we do not treat well. If they are not so positioned, they must be seen in an even worse light as an evil character.

***

Editor's note: Sadly, this chapter was incomplete at the time of Val Plumwood's death.

Second section

4. A wombat wake: In memoriam Birubi

My wombat Birubi died after a brief illness sometime around Wednesday 18 August 1999. I miss Birubi greatly and continue to catch his beloved form (or 'ghost') out of the corner of my eye, a half-seen image flitting around the corner of a cupboard or across the veranda. Long after his death, my eyes continued to search out his shape on the moonlit grass. He was part of my life for so long—over twelve years—that I found it hard to believe he would no longer wait for me or greet me, that he was finally gone.

We had a wake for him a few days later. The idea of the wake was to focus on his life rather than his death, to honour presence rather than mourn absence, and to celebrate and express gratitude for Birubi's life and for wombat life more generally. We had a small ceremony for him, and told many Birubi stories and wombat stories generally. Many of the people who helped care for Birubi over the years when I was working overseas or in distant parts of Australia were present with their own experiences and thoughts to contribute. The wake was far from being a dismal occasion. Birubi had a full and whole wombat life and died what seemed to be a dignified and peaceful wombat death. He came to the house for sanctuary in his final months and often rested or slept in front of the fire, but returned to his burrow, snug pouch of mother earth, in his last hours.

Birubi came to me from the wildlife rescue service as a malnourished and very sick orphan. His mother had probably died of the mange, a disease introduced by Europeans with their dogs that brings so many wombats to an early and tormented death. Since my own human son had recently died, Birubi and I bonded strongly. Birubi (the name, meaning I believe 'the drum', was given him by his first carers in the rescue service) was about a year old, furred but still suckling, when he took up residence with me. He seemed to have suffered greatly from his mother's death and was desperate for care.

Birubi had received from his wombat mother a good quality wombat education; she had taught him to defecate outside the burrow (or its equivalent, my house), and the rudiments of survival in the bush. Within a day of arriving he learnt to open the sliding glass doors of the house and could go outside into the bush whenever he wished (which was often). His ability to control the access between his world and mine enabled him to be active in choosing and structuring the balance between us, to enter my world while still fully retaining his wombatness. He was generally wary of humans until he had clearly established their identity, and would exit the house if it was too noisy or unsettling.

Birubi grew to belong to both the world of the house and that of the forest, supposedly exclusive and mutually oppositional. He needed a lot of medical treatment and supplementary feeding for the first year, so he became accustomed to the house and knew something of its comforts. But from the beginning he was based primarily out of doors in various holes he selected or renovated, and always preferred that world. Once established in his own nearby burrows in the forest, he came to the house on a visiting basis on the average for an hour or so most evenings for personal, moral and material support. (At his behest I supplemented his grazing with carrots and rolled oats, which corresponded to the roots and seeds sections of the wombat diet). In the first year he would spend part of the night out of doors, and part in my bed with me. He initiated all these high contact arrangements, and would not easily be turned aside from them, (although since wombats are nocturnal, they often led to me getting inadequate sleep). Sometimes I had to exclude him by locking the doors if he became too demanding of my time or arrived at very unreasonable hours.

To sleep next to me was his ardent desire, but it presented some difficulties. It was wise to get the leeches and ticks off him before letting him into the bed if you wanted a comfortable rest. After I had got into bed, he would come over and start biting its edge furiously until I gave him a hand up. Once in bed, he would usually lie down next to me on his side and drop off like a light. I can attest that during sleep he often ground his teeth and also vocalised in ways that suggested the imaginary encounters of dreaming. Usually he would wake up again about two hours later and go outside to graze, (and of course I was then obliged to get up to close the door he left open in case dangerous or unsuitable animals entered).

Since he was a skilful door and cupboard opener, Birubi had to be locked out of the house when there was nobody else there. There are many stories about what happened when Birubi got into the house without supervision. He was very skilful with his mouth, which he used for manipulation and encounter, and enjoyed opening and exploring food packages and biting hard furniture and soft stuffed things. His tastes are commemorated around my house on cushions, chairs, stools, hassocks and cupboard doors.

Birubi was a vigorous player of various wombat chasing and hiding games he began to teach me as soon as he recovered his strength. These games seemed to me (there is of course much uncertainty here) to roll together features of play, love and war. He played very rough by human standards, but I do not think that he really intended to hurt—it's probably just that wombats are tougher, especially around the ankles, his favourite nipping point when he caught you. He was a skilful game player who expected to win, would sulk if he did not, and had learnt the efficacy of feinting. When young, Birubi would have been happy I think to play games all day, but fortunately this desire waned a bit as he grew older. Even as an older wombat, though, he showed that he liked a game and had a sense of humour.

I was always conscious of a dimension of mystery in my knowledge of Birubi's mind. The sense of bridging a great gulf of difference was part of the magic of the relationship. I think it was the centrality of the mother–child relationship to both our species and what was shared in its framework of ethics and expectations that made possible intimate contact with a creature so very different. This kind of relationship is necessarily cast in communicative terms that disrupt the severely restricted vocabulary for describing animal behaviour and interaction allowed by reductionist science and its objectivist ideals of non-relationship or its near approximation, subject–object relationship. Although you could entertain a large range of hypotheses about the meaning, complexity and specificity of his responses, that relationship, plus your knowledge of context and past interactions, usually suggested some credible and reasonably lucid tale about the other's mental processes and attitudes that enabled you to continue relating as co-actors in a partially shared narrative of the world. There were times, especially when he was an adolescent testing out his power, when I felt my relationship with him was balanced on a knife edge, but as he matured it took on a less precarious form.

Birubi, like other wombats and unlike dogs, was a resilient and determined animal who could not be shaped to human will. He did not recognise human superiority or pretensions to own the world and had a strong sense of his own independent selfhood, his own equal interests and entitlements. This stubbornness and sense of equality is the feature that has brought the wombat so strongly into conflict with the farmer, but to me it was wonderful. It meant that you were dealing with a real other; that contact had to be on his terms and not just on yours. Discipline, punishment and training to accept human will, of the sort we apply to dogs, were out of the question; not only would they be totally ineffective, but they would jeopardise the entire basis of relationship.

Once you had recognised that he would not give way to you, you were motivated to find creative ways to work around conflict or to give way yourself. A corollary of his independence was his anger when thwarted. Birubi tended to get quite angry if shut out of the house or the veggie patch, would snort in a loud disgusted tone and sometimes retaliate destructively, for example by chewing the doormat or digging a big hole in front of the garden gate. As primarily a grass eater, he rarely did much harm in the veggie garden though (except for digging up the carrots). He did not usually hold a grudge for long, although there were a few occasions when he was still angry with me the next day for something I had done the day before.

Wombats, being burrow dwellers, like a few home comforts. Birubi liked to sit (and in his latter days especially sleep) right in front of the wood stove in midwinter. He was fascinated by the fire and used to poke his nose right up against the hot glass until it hurt (something he never learnt not to do). He was very partial to a hot bum rub, and loved to stand in front of the stove rubbing his rear end against the warm corner. Birubi's sexual expression began while he was still quite young and only subsided in the last few years of his life. He was erotically aroused by cushions, and would attempt to copulate with them after a fifteen-minute foreplay period of savage biting. He was often absent for considerable periods, especially in the warmer months, and several times I came across him miles away. I speculate that he may have been away visiting wombat lovers. If so I hope he treated them better than he did the cushions.

Because wombats are solitary and do not form family groups, I know little of Birubi's relationships with other wombats, with the exception of his male rival Clancy. Clancy lived about two kilometres away but would often come over for a feed and a fight. He was openly envious of Birubi's privileges in relation to humans and wanted them for himself (and himself alone). Birubi had to face up to Clancy's aggression when he was still a juvenile, and was valiant in the face of Clancy's superior age, size and fighting skills. Nevertheless when I heard the sounds of warfare between Clancy and Birubi (a high pitched, harsh call), I would run out and try to separate the combatants and bring peace and light, but was sometimes unable to prevent the infliction of some nasty wounds, mainly to Birubi.

The strife between Birubi and Clancy placed me in a painful conflict between wombat ethical systems and human ones. Should I give my favour to the stronger, as Clancy clearly hoped, or use my superior strength to help and sustain the 'wombat son' I was so attached to? I found this a difficult moral dilemma, since Clancy was the indigenous occupant, but in the end resolved it in the same way as most human mothers, trying to honour commitment to protect the one near and dear to me while avoiding injustice towards his enemy.

Birubi was wily, wary and tough, but the forest is a dangerous place. Sometimes Birubi's fear of what lay outside the door was palpable. I could not protect him, and every time he left the house I knew that he might be badly injured or that I might never see him again. So the relationship was painful as well as joyful, just as it is for the many human mothers who are powerless to prevent harm to the children they love. Birubi was in great fear of dogs, the privileged gatekeeper animals who are allowed and even encouraged to terrorise the others, and he would often avoid my company, sometimes for a week or so, if I had been to lunch at the house of someone who owned a dog. (I think if people realised what terror and danger they cause to sensitive wild animals like Birubi and those who care about them they would be much more careful about owning and restraining dogs.) This is an example of the great depth of temporal understanding available to those who possess a well-developed olfactory form of knowledge.

Birubi was an intelligent herbivore, a vegetarian, I believe, in the full sense, both through his biological inheritance and through his convictions. As a non-meat-eater myself, I had a rare opportunity to observe his opinions on meat eating when a friend came to stay bringing with them a dog they fed normally on fresh mutton on the bone. I watched Birubi carefully inspecting and sniffing the site where the dog ate its flesh meals and examining a partly consumed bone. He gave every sign of horror, and came to the house only infrequently and with the greatest reluctance while the dog and the meat smell remained around. On another occasion, when I had fresh minced meat on my hands from feeding an injured juvenile magpie, he backed away from me with obvious revulsion and did not return until several days later when the odour was gone.

Reduced sexual expression was one of a number of signs of aging in Birubi's last few years, which included the greying of his beautiful soft coat and the general reduction in his energy and vigour as indicated by his lessened interest in games and play. At age 13 he was one of the oldest wombats the wildcare people had heard of. I put this down mainly to my five kilometre distance from the nearest road, the automobile being such a major cause of wombat carnage. Wombats have been known to live to 25 years in captivity, and if Birubi aged prematurely in these terms it could reflect an unknown disease process or the extreme rigours of the early period of his life.

I feel it was an incredible privilege to be allowed to know a free, wary and basically wild animal so intimately and richly. Our relationship cut across the usual boundary between the wild and domestic, the forest and the house, the non-human and the human, nature and culture. The 'culture' world is understood to be a humanised world in which identities are assimilated to the human and conformed to human will, interests and standards. In this world the 'good dog' is part of human culture, trained to accept human dominance and human terms, (terms made possible by the canine social system to be sure but still set by humans), rather than to interact as an equal party bringing their own independent terms. On the other side, the 'nature' world is one we in the West tend now to see mainly through the instrumental and reductionist framework of 'detached' science that tries to delegitimate the rich personal knowledge of highly developed individual caring relationships.

It is no coincidence that the more revolutionary forms of ethology pioneered by women like Jane Goodall have given us new insights precisely because they have broken these false choices down. Between them, the 'nature' and 'culture' frameworks rule out the possibility of deep personal contact with animals except on our terms. Birubi was a 'wild familiar' who established his own terms for contact and friendship. It was an enormous thrill to explore forms of contact that transgressed the nature/culture boundary, so constitutive of our civilisation. It was enchanting, the enchantment of childhood imagination and story, to walk side by side with Birubi along a forest track, to look up from my desk to find a forest-dwelling wombat sitting in my armchair by the fire. You had the courage and freedom to cross the boundary, Birubi. But do we?

Ave atque vale, Birubi. We will remember you.

5. 'Babe': The tale of the speaking meat

Part I

"You look a little shy: let me introduce you to that leg of mutton," said the Red Queen. "Alice — Mutton: Mutton — Alice."

The leg of mutton got up in the dish and made a little bow to Alice, and Alice returned the bow, not knowing whether to be frightened or amused.

"May I give you a slice?" she said, taking up the knife and fork, and looking from one Queen to the other.

"Certainly not," the Red Queen said, very decidedly: "it isn't etiquette to cut anyone you've been introduced to. Remove the joint!"

Alice through the looking glass, pp. 132–133.

The unprejudiced heart

I would like somebody somewhere to endow an annual prize for a work of art which takes a group of the most oppressed subjects and makes an effective and transformative representation of their situation. The work would make its audience care about what happens to those oppressed subjects and to understand something of the audience's own role in maintaining their oppression. It would foster recognition of the subjectivity and creativity of the oppressed group and consciousness of the need for redistribution of respect and of cultural and material goods. Above all, it would help to support and protect them. If these are subjects who are conventionally seen as radically excluded, for example as beyond the possibility of communication or as embodied in ways which occasion aversion or anxiety, the prize work should attempt to disrupt those violence-prone perceptions.

One of my nominations for such a prize would be the film *Babe*. Before seeing the film, I would have doubted that it was possible to make a highly successful film for mass audiences that could do those things for one of the most oppressed subjects in our society, the meat pig. One feature that made this achievement possible was that the film successfully disrupted the adult/child boundary and created space for adults to share certain kinds of openness to and sympathy for animals permitted to children but normally out of bounds for mature adults. This is one of the devices which enables the film, like Dick King-Smith's prize-winning book *The Sheep–Pig* on which it is based,[1] to succeed to a remarkable degree in opening for the pig the 'unprejudiced heart' invoked in the narrator's opening sentence. It is not just the film's problematisation of the concept of meat that makes this film philosophically interesting; it also poses ethical and political questions, analogous to some of those arising in post-colonial theory, about the distinction between meat and non-meat animals and about the role of the human contract with those special more privileged 'pet' animals who can never be 'meat'.

Because the main theme of *Babe* turns around the refusal of communicative status to animals, the film is of considerable interest for philosophical accounts of human–animal relations. The story provides a rich context for thinking about this communicative status, posing questions about the inadequacy of narrow rationalist accounts of communication, about representations of animal communication and the charge of anthropomorphism, and about the contradictions and paradoxes disclosed when we recognise *the meat* as a communicative subject. *Babe* repeatedly problematises the kind of prejudice that relegates the other to a sphere of radical otherness marked by rational deficiency, mechanistic reduction and exclusion from communicative status. The pig Babe disrupts the assumption that because he is a meat animal, he is 'too stupid to understand'; the story problematises the sheep–dog Fly's dismissal of sheep-talk as 'just so much rubbish, to which she never paid any attention'. The refusal of communicative status to animals is a crucial, formative arena where closure and exclusion strategies which affect many humans are developed and perfected. *Babe* thus provides many insights into closure strategies as they affect both humans and non-humans.

Babe also offers a recognition of communicative virtues and characteristics as central to both human and non-human forms of life, and offers a vision of the emergence of communicative forms of relationship as victorious alternatives to forms based on violence, domination and terror. The film does not suggest any exploration of the ethical and political ambiguities of communicative forms, which are potentially rather more compatible with oppression than it suggests, and are implicated in the replacement of repressive patriarchal models by hegemonic models based on the master subject, as in certain forms of liberal democratic politics for example. But as Dryzek and Plumwood[2] have argued, communicative models of relationships with nature and animals seem likely to offer us a better chance of survival in the difficult times ahead than dominant mechanistic models which promote insensitivity to the others' agency and denial of our dependency on them. *Babe* crystallises in a useful way a clash of models that is critical for our times.

---

1   Dick King-Smith, *The sheep–pig*, Harmondsworth Middlesex, Puffin Books, 1983.
2   John Dryzek, *Discursive democracy*, Cambridge, Cambridge University Press, 1990 and Val Plumwood, *Feminism and the mastery of nature*, London, Routledge, 1993.

My initial reason for going to the movie however had much more to do with being homesick—I was away from Australia for a long period and the film had been shot in a shire near my home. I hoped to hear again the sounds of the bush—those small but intensely evocative background calls—especially the local birds and frogs which appear in the background on most soundtracks—that creep up on you unawares to create powerful longings for a much-loved place. But when I took my seat in the darkened cinema, something else made me cry too, with sorrow and shame for my own complicity in the dominant cultural tradition of rational human mastery over animals and nature—as well as everything else considered beneath the master realm of reason. These were the powerful opening scenes of *Babe* showing the terrible cruelty of the intensive pig farms in which the pig Babe, treated as living meat, is introduced to us as narrative subject.

These visions of hell took on special power and poignancy for me because at the time I saw the film I was living in the second highest US state for intensive hog production. The state of North Carolina was a place where one rarely saw farm animals out in the open and many of the rivers and estuaries were seriously degraded or under assault from the toxic run-off generated by the intensive factory farms. Many of the huge pig 'slaughter facilities' in the US employ largely prison labour. The work of those who labour on the killing floor of these massive facilities slaughtering up to 15,000 pigs a day is so terrible and poorly paid that only the slave-like workforce of the carceral system, or those coerced by other forms of desperation such as indentured immigrants, are available as workers. The concentration camps too employed some categories of prisoners to organise, imprison and execute others. The treatment of the pigs and that of the prisoners has much in common; in both cases, the intense segregation of the gulag ensures that the middle class rarely has to confront the hidden connection between its ugly and violent reality and their own comfortable and tidy lives. The speech of both pigs and prisoners is erased or delegitimated, and both are reduced to living meat. As C. Stone Brown argues, 'African Americans are the flesh that maintains a profitable "prison industry"'.[3] As disciplinary democracy normalises massive incarceration, and more of us become either prisoners or keepers, the fate of non-human and human prisoners increasingly converges.

The nightmarish opening scenes of *Babe* showed an ugly gulag reality that was all around but which was banished from thought and sight, and generally treated, even by the animal liberation movement, as too well established for serious contest. In these circumstances, who could avoid being immediately caught up in the little pig's plight, or avoid comparing the misery of the incarcerated animals with the consumptive pleasures of the over-privileged humans the next shots cut to? The filmic technique at this point had us crossing that crucial

3   C. Stone Brown, 'Prison guards fund governor for presidential race', *Z Magazine*, Sept/October 1995.

animal/human subject boundary with dizzying speed, so fast that our usual distancing defences did not have time to cut in and tell us that these subjects are not at all comparable, that humans count and pigs don't. Who could avoid comparing the pigs' misery with the humans' pleasure, or avoid thoughts of concentration camps and gas chambers as the pig mothers were torn from their children and cattle-prodded into that terrible night journey from which there was no return?

The answer, of course, to this question is: 'quite a lot of people'. Many people didn't see animals or animal liberation as the topic of the film, and some reviewers seemed to think it was all about how you could cross gender and class boundaries and burst categories to make yourself anything you wanted to be, even a sheep–pig, if you had enough determination and willpower—a sophisticated postmodern–neoliberal Animal Farm allegory about personal responsibility, individual merit rewarded, and trying harder. *Babe* does have valid things to say to a human audience about not staying in the boxes convention puts you into, but the message here is also relevant to breaking down hierarchies of considerability which serve to confine non-humans. And the inability to see how animals themselves could be a serious topic for such a film is an indicator of their assigned status as beneath subjectivity and seriousness, both effective defences against hearing the story of the speaking meat that *Babe* articulates. The pig Babe speaks from the most delegitimated subject position possible in our society, that of the meat, and we have developed strategies for blocking out and not hearing the speech of those in that position. We could not continue the sorts of meat practices the pig–human gulag system is based upon without these kinds of strategies. One of the great strengths of the film is that it invites us to challenge some of these paradoxes, blocks and erasures.

The paradox of the speaking meat

In the opening scenes of the factory farm we are introduced to the piglet Babe as the film's main narrative subject (marked by the subject's theme on the soundtrack, among other marks of subjecthood). We open with a shot showing real piglets waking in expressive communication, and then see one of these meat-subjects expressing his/her[4] sorrow at the loss of his mother, and his fear as he is seized by strangers and carried away to be raffled. As his mother is prodded into the truck, Babe utters his grief so fleetingly and naturally that we hardly notice that our usual assumptions have been turned on their heads. The meat animal is being presented to us as an expressive, narrative subject—the meat is speaking. There are several disruptions here. What is disrupted immediately

---

4   I have assumed the masculine pronoun here for Babe because this is used in King-Smith 1983, but the film is more ambiguous on this point.

is the Cartesian model of the machine–animal, the dominant model which enables the ontological presence, mind-like and communicative characteristics of animals to be so utterly denied in the factory farm, where their entire lives are defined and distorted by the function of serving human appetite. There is paradox in the concept of speaking meat *Babe* confronts us with, precisely because the concept of meat totally erases that speaking position; there is no possibility of encountering the meat as expressive, narrative subject.

An inquiry into the concept of meat provides a useful route into understanding how 'taxonomy' connects ontology with ethics—how certain strategies of representation normalise oppression by narrowing ethically relevant perception, erasing key ethical dimensions of situations, and sometimes even making the Other complicit in their own oppression through internalising oppressive forms of identity. As Carol Adams has argued, the concept of meat justifies oppression by hiding responsibility for death and the causal connection between the production of meat and the animal's death.[5] The backgrounding, erasure or denial of these connections in the abstractly quantitative and commodified concept of meat Adams terms 'absent referent'. 'Absent referent' involves a complex process of splitting that renders unavailable not only the act of killing which makes meat available as a commodity, but any recognition of connection between the meat and those who consume it. To achieve this the concept of meat must simultaneously establish several profound splits or radical exclusions, between process–product, mind–body, and us–them. The first of these involves a radical dissociation which denies the connection between the processes set in motion by our intentions and the end product of commodified, quantitatively specifiable flesh. The second radically dissociates the subjectivity which sets these processes in motion from that of its victim, denying their kinship as socially connected, purposive and communicative beings, and presenting the victim reductively as flesh. 'You looks at us,' says King-Smith's wise old sheep Ma; 'and you sees lamb chops'.

The third background assumption involved in modern industrial society's concept of meat as commodity denies the possibility of human consumers themselves ever taking the form of meat, by a background assumption of a hierarchy of use and considerability which is linked to an alleged hierarchy of mental and communicative capacities between species, with humans of course at the top. These assumptions together make the ideas of 'human meat' almost as unthinkable a possibility as that of being introduced to the speaking meat. The concept of meat is a form of life[6] (Wittgenstein 1954) in which taxonomy structures our moral vision via the ethical and epistemological possibilities it

---

5   Carol Adams, *The sexual politics of meat*, New York, Continuum, 1994.
6   Ludwig Wittgenstein, *Philosophical investigations*, Oxford, Blackwell, 1954.

discloses or denies.[7] These sets of background denials enable the presentation of the other in the instrumental terms that Marilyn Frye has identified as belonging to the arrogant perspective in which viewers 'organise everything seen with reference to themselves and their own interests',[8] in this case, in terms of a strong instrumental reductionism which identifies the other with what is only a part of their being, the part that is of use to us as flesh. Since we, in contrast, are identified as humans in terms which emphasise, rather than suppress or deny, our subjectivity, and which tend to background our bodily aspects of identity, beings identified as meat become radically Other: not only can we never be included in the category of meat ourselves, we can never be introduced to the meat.

There is injustice in each of these modes of conception. There is injustice for a communicative and ethical being in being conceived systematically in ways that refuse recognition of this status and these characteristics. There is injustice for such a being in being conceived reductively as body, first because such conception singles its referent out for treatment as radically less than it is, and second because such an instrumental reductionism defines the Other in terms that assume the right of a 'higher' group to treat them as a resource for their ends. Animals so conceived are subject to both radical exclusion (as having a radically different nature discontinuous from that of the human meat consumer) and homogenisation—they 'drown in the anonymous collectivity' of the commodity form meat. The radical exclusion aspect of the meat concept denies kinship and generates a conceptual distance or boundary between humanity and its 'meat' which blocks sympathy, reduces the risk of identification with those so designated, and silences them as communicative beings. The reductiveness of the meat concept permits a conceptual strategy designed to block recognition of these injustices, and its disruption in the concept of the speaking meat is one source of the flavour of paradox that lingers around that idea.

But from the injustice of industrial society's institution of meat as commodity, and the moral cowardice and evasion of the associated conceptual strategies of denial, we cannot conclude that there is no moral alternative to a universalised vegetarianism, that there are no other, less ethically problematic ways to resolve the tensions between conceiving non-humans both as communicative others and as food. In the complex biological exchange which sustains all our lives, we must all gain sustenance at the expense of the other, 'the one living the other's

---

7 This is one reason why the task of obtaining an adequate environmental and non-anthrocentric ethic should not be equated with that of enunciating abstract principles of equal treatment and extending them to non-human others. Anthrocentric taxonomy will always defeat abstract moral principles, however comprehensive.

8 Marilyn Frye, *The politics of reality*, New York, The Crossing Press, p. 67.

death, and dying the other's life', in the words of Heraclitus. Shagbark Hickory outlines an alternative, non-reductive perspective on this exchange which does not refuse the moral complexities and perplexities involved:

For most or all American Indians food (plant as well as animal) is kin. Relationships to plants and animals as, on the one hand, food and, on the other hand, kin creates a tension which is dealt with mythically, ritually, and ceremonially, but which is never denied. It is this refusal to deny the dilemma in which we are implicated in this life, a refusal to take the way of bad faith, moral supremacy, or self-deception which constitutes a radical challenge to our relationships to our food. The American Indian view that considerability goes "all the way down" requires a response considerably more sophisticated than those we have seen in the West, which consist either in drawing lines of moral considerability in order to create an out-group, or in constructing hierarchies of considerability creating de facto out-groups in particular cases.[9]

Many forms of vegetarianism remain trapped in the Western strategies of denial and radical exclusion which create further out-groups, merely redrawing the boundary of otherness in a different place, at the border of animality rather than humanity. In contrast, the indigenous recognition that the central philosophical problem of human life is that '*all* our food is souls' points towards non-reductive practices and understandings of food that resolve the moral failings of 'bad faith, moral supremacy, [and] self-deception' Shagbark Hickory finds implicit in the dominant Western meat concept. However, to the extent that these alternative understandings of food form part of a different 'form of life', in Wittgenstein's sense,[10] they are not readily available, either practically or conceptually, within the context of contemporary industrial life and its commodified food relationships. Conversely, the fact that vegetarianism may usually be the course which, in the context of such a commodity society, will best minimise our complicity in injustice towards others does nothing to support the Eurocentric conclusion that vegetarianism is a universal moral requirement for all people in all societies in all situations.[11]

The paradox of the speaking meat is both the product of a particular social context, and a powerful symptom of some of the most indicative moral failings of that context. The Western solution to the moral dilemmas of food is the creation of a set of moral dualisms, involving a sharp discontinuity between those who deserve and those who are beyond ethical consideration.

---

9   Shagbark Hickory, 'Environmental etiquette/environmental practice: American Indian challenges to mainstream environmental ethics', in Max Oelschlaeger ed. *The company of others: Essays in celebration of Paul Shephard*, Durango, Colorado, Kivaki Press, 1995.
10   See Wittgenstein, 1954.
11   Carol Adams, *The sexual politics of meat* and 'Ecofeminism and the eating of animals', *Hypatia*, Vol. 6 No. 1, 1991, pp. 125–145.

As we have seen, the speaking meat forces us to confront the way this moral dualism and discontinuity is based on reductionism, denial and silencing. Our civilisation's orientation to the creation of moral dualisms may be one reason for its technological dominance, since it removes any constraints of respect which might otherwise hold back development, but it remains a major source of corruption of our ethical practices. The silencing solutions of moral dualism are always potentially capable of extension to selected groups of humans counted as lesser in their humanity, and we have seen this extension made many times in this century. This silencing possibility is always present, of course, in any human society, but it is greatly reinforced by the entrenchment of the dualist model in the basic case of food.

The communicative model

The overarching model which subsumes the commodity model of the animal and its specific modes of and motives for reduction is the Cartesian–mechanistic reduction of the non-human animal to its body, and the associated refusal to recognise non-human animals as akin to human ones in the possession of mind, intention and communication. Mary Midgley and Barbara Noske[12] are two philosophers who have pointed out that the moral failings implicit in the modern, commodified concept of meat find their philosophical progenitor in Cartesian rationalism and the mechanistic model. The rationalist–mechanistic model of the animal is a key part of the relation between modernity and the non-human world, and its rationality is expressed both in reductive concepts like meat and in the practices of the factory farm. The mechanistic model erases the possibility of communication by denying mind-like properties to non-humans; ideals of manipulation and instrumental rationality are at odds with communicative ideals and with the conception of the other as a communicative subject. *Babe* confronts us with the conflict between the mechanistic model of the factory farm, and the communicative model of human/animal relations the film ultimately vindicates. This alternative communicative model is located in the film in the romantically presented contrast space of the Hoggett's family farm, where it struggles to emerge in the unconventional role tolerated for the former meat animal Babe and Babe's communicative reformation of relationships with the sheep. But the farm itself is the site of conflict between the communicative and the Cartesian–reductive models, for it too contains the meat house and the animal regimes based on fear and force. The conflict between these models is also represented in the form of the conflict within the taciturn farmer and between him and the more conventional farm wife.

---

12   Margaret Midgley, *Animals and why they matter*, London, Penguin, 1983 and Barbara Noske, *Humans and other animals*, London, Pluto Press, 1989.

Nevertheless, animal liberationists have some justification for viewing the film's major implicit contrast between the factory farm and the family farm with a sceptical eye. To say that the family farm setting of *Babe* is highly romanticised is an understatement. A cynic might say that the family farm parallels the family as the site of mystifying representations and idealisations. The contrasts of *Babe* hide the fact that the family farm model is compatible with, and normally involves, many oppressive animal husbandry practices; the destination of most of its animal food-producing units is ultimately the market, and all that has changed is the indoor setting. This would be, I think, to ignore the fact that moral differences of degree can be important; it would be like saying that there is no moral difference between being a worker on a production line and an inmate of a concentration camp, because both involve some degree of reduction and instrumentalisation. If there is a moral difference between the smaller scale farm and the animal gulag, however, there is also normally a lot more continuity than *Babe* makes visible.

But to dismiss the implicit contrast of *Babe* in this way would be to miss the point that *Babe* also makes visible a new possibility—the possibility of replacing a dominant model of mechanistic relations by a communicative one which recognises the animal's status as a communicative and moral being and revolutionises the moral basis of relationships with domestic animals. Whether this is compatible with farming as we know it remains an open question, but one the film deserves credit for raising. *Babe* leaves us in no doubt that meat is violence, and it posits a model of communication in opposition to that violence, and hence a new vision of relations to domestic animals. It does not explore the puzzles in that vision, leaving us with various paradoxes to chew on. But its communicative model presents a final vision of some power, including the triumph of the communicative skills and ethic Babe has acquired from the maternal wisdom of the sheep and various other proxy mothers.

Babe's status as a communicative subject has received so little attention in the monstrous regime of the gulag that he does not even have an individual name. But, as we soon discover when Babe is removed through the device of the raffle to the relatively enlightened world of the family farm, Babe's status as a communicative subject still has many obstacles to overcome to gain recognition. Before arrival at the farm, Babe is initially just a 'worthless little runt', an object to be weighed, raffled off and eaten. In the idealised world of the Hoggett's traditional farm, Babe's communicative capacities are initially dimly, then more clearly, recognised by Farmer Hoggett. But they are not initially recognised by his wife, who addresses him as 'you lucky little pork chop' and looks forward to Babe's transformation into the familiar commodity form of 'two nice hams, two sides of bacon, pork chops, kidneys, liver, chitterling, trotters etc'.

The film version of Mrs. Hoggett, unlike the book version, is made to represent the most closed, convention and consumer-bound version of the human character.[13] Although this elaboration of conflicting perspectives adds some richness to the film's themes and characterisation, the linking of the conflict between the mechanistic and communicative perspectives in this way with gender introduces elements of androcentrism into the story, obscures the real connections between gender and consumerism and between gender and the mechanistic model,[14] and generates contradictory messages about the affirmation of animality. This emerges in the film's derogatory representation of the farm wife in animalistic terms and in the implicit demeaning of women's understanding and tasks as consumeristic and materialistic, in contrast to the more 'spiritual' orientation of the farmer/father. Babe's subjectivity is recognised by several animal foster mothers, the dog Fly and the sheep Maa, who develop babe's communicative and social abilities in the best maternal traditions. But although Babe's unusual communicative abilities must ultimately derive from these various mothers (who must have included the original pig mother he missed so much), it is their completion and recognition by the father/farmer, represented as the 'unprejudiced heart', that are positioned in the movies as the key transformative elements for Babe and for the culture more generally.

The farmer is, for reasons the film leaves unexplored, open to certain possibilities of animal communication the others around him are closed to. By various communicative deeds, babe gradually earns the farmer's recognition of his subjectivity, or so he believes, but is devastated by the final – incredible – discovery of his status as meat, revealed to him by the jealous cat. This apparent betrayal, (of almost biblical proportions) by the father, almost kills Babe, who like the duck Ferdie, cannot bear to live as only meat. At this point in the story, as at the beginning and the end, Babe is positioned as a Christ figure, the feminised, dependent son who is affirmed and revived by the farmer/father's recognition and love, expressed in the dance of life. Together Babe and farmer go on to accomplish the apparently impossible feat of opening closed minds and demonstrating Babe's unrecognised communicative ability to the world. We are invited to conclude that this revolutionises the treatment of pigs and of farming generally, reformulating it as an activity based on communication rather than force and violence. The communicative ethic is also strongly represented by the (female) sheep, whose persistent faith in and exemplification of the virtues and values of communication and non-violence is essential to their ultimate victory over the reductive violence of traditional relationships.

---

13   In King-Smith 1983, Mrs Hoggett is the first to fully recognise Babe's contributions and to invite him into the house, explicitly admitting him to the contract class.
14   Especially since feminists have argued that the mechanistic models which deny communicative power to nature represent a masculinist response to growing technological mastery, among other things. See for example Merchant 1980.

Communicative relationships open up new moral possibilities for organising life in ways that can negotiate conflicts of interests, build agreement, trust and mutuality, and avoid instrumentalism and the imposition of the will of one party on the other by force. Communicative relations don't necessarily follow out those possibilities however, and it is important not to romanticise the communicative model, which does not automatically eliminate the dynamic of power, either in terms of equality of access, of hierarchy in forms of communication, or of the structuring of communication in hegemonic ways. There are various strategies for taking back the greater equality communicative models appear to offer. Rationalist models which treat communication as an exercise in pure, abstract, neutral and universal reason, and which delegitimate the more emotional and bodily forms and aspects of communication, operate to exclude non-humans from full communicative status just as they exclude various human others accorded lower human status as further from the rational ideal. These rationalist models exclude the forms of communication associated with animals along with the forms of communication associated with women, with non-Western cultures and with less 'educated' classes.[15]

Communicative models which allow us to overcome these exclusions for humans will also help us to recognise non-human animals in their denied aspects as communicative beings, but an excessive emphasis on communication and its use as a criterion of moral worth or value would remain problematic for non-humans in basing itself on a capacity which may still be highly characteristic of humanity, and in biasing our valuations heavily towards those species most similar to ourselves. To overcome this implicit anthrocentrism, a communicative model would need to be part of a plural set of grounds for valuation, rather than its unique and exclusive basis, and to be sensitive to communicative capacities within species as well as to their capacities for communication with humans.

If the film's communicative vision offers hope of moving on to a new stage beyond mechanism, it also leaves us with many tantalising questions about this new stage which arise from the ambivalence of communication. Will communication be on our terms or theirs? Will Babe's communicative abilities be used for the good of the animals or for that of the farmer? If the film's account of the moral development of 'the farmer (reaching its climax in the step-dance) offers a vision of the small farm as a putative future enterprise of love and communication with nature and animals, the film also casts little light on the question of what the communicative farm would be like. Will the new communicative paradigm be used to liberate the sheep and the other farm animals, or merely to oppress them in more subtle and self-complicit ways? Will the communicative animal farm stand to the mechanistic farm as the hegemonic communicative forms of liberal

---

15   Iris Young, 'Communication and the other: Beyond deliberative democracy,' in Margaret Wilson and Anna Yeatman, eds, *Justice and identity: Antipodean practices*, Sydney, Allen and Unwin, 1995, pp. 134–152.

democracy stand to the more repressive forms of patriarchal–authoritarian governance they replaced? The distinction between democracy and despotism is supposedly built on such a contrast, but as it becomes increasingly clear how little our own society resembles the democratic ideal of free and open dialogue to which all have access, it also becomes clear how our communicative abilities can be used to control and imprison us. A new communicative stage of human–nature relationships would need to place such questions at the centre of its critical thought: at this level, the tale of the speaking meat has only just begun.

Part II

Communication and anthropomorphism

Babe's opening shot shows Babe waking in communicative interaction with siblings, expressing sorrow at the loss of his mother and fear as he is seized and carried away. These are all emotions we can realistically expect real pigs to feel and express in this situation, and Babe's 'human' speech as it emerges in this context seems a natural expression of these emotions, wishes and beliefs. The animal communication introduced here works well because it continues and extends the normal body language and communication of the animals. Nevertheless, the representation of such animal subjectivity in human terms is often said to be irresolvably problematic and invalidly 'anthropomorphic'. It is worth considering and clarifying this charge in relation to the representation of animal communication and subjectivity in works of art.

We need to distinguish various senses of anthropomorphism, including general and specific senses. The general concept and charge of anthropomorphism, as Mary Midgley has argued, is in its usual sense and definition thoroughly confused.[16] It is ambiguous as between attributing to non-humans characteristics humans have (OED), and attributing to non-humans characteristics *only* humans have. Both senses are problematic, in slightly different ways, when used to support the claim that the attribution of characteristics such as subjectivity to animals must be anthropomorphic. The first sense, that something is anthropomorphic if it attributes to animals characteristics humans have, implies that there is no overlap of characteristics between humans and non-human animals. That is, it assumes a duality of human and animal natures and attempts to enforce upon legitimate representations of non-humans such a radical discontinuity. This sense should clearly be rejected, not only because it is based on a demonstrably

---

16   Mary Midgley, *Animals and why they matter*, London, Penguin, 1983.

false assumption of radical discontinuity, but because it could be used to delegitimate virtually any depiction of non-human subjectivity that made sense to us.

The second sense of anthropomorphism—attributing to non-humans characteristics only humans have—is not open to this objection, but is open to the objection that its use to delegitimate the attribution of subjectivity and other contested characteristics to non-humans is simply question-begging. It assumes just what is at issue, what opponents of the mechanistic model contest, that non-humans do *not* have characteristics such as subjectivity and intentionality humans also possess. And furthermore, such a sense is otiose and human-centred. If a representation attributes to non-humans characteristics they do not have, that provides (in a strictly veridical context) sufficient independent ground for rejecting such an attribution. It is simply anthrocentric to go on to add that humans do have such characteristics, and to focus on this as the grounds for error. There is no good basis for the general claim that an artwork is invalidated by anthropomorphism just because it attributes subjectivity and communication to non-humans in a general way.

Nevertheless, there may still a point in more specific and limited senses and charges of anthropomorphism. One sense of anthropomorphism we might appeal to here would be analogous to, say, certain ways of rejecting Eurocentrism which object to representing the non-European other in terms of a European norm. This sense would enable an argument that the mode of representation adopted in particular, specific cases denied the difference of animals and represented them in terms of a human model. The argument would be that, although animals do have subjectivity and do communicate, the representation of that communication in the terms of human speech adopted by a film like *Babe* is invalidly anthropomorphic, depicted in excessively human terms.

One problem with this argument is that, although it looks as if this sense appeals to a concept of anthropomorphism different from the objectionable general one, it is in danger of degenerating into a similarly general form. To bring this out, we need to ask, what is the contrast class? What mode of representing animal subjectivity or communication, beyond its bare recording without any attempt to convey a meaning or place in the animal's life (as in commentary-free films of wolves howling or whales making sounds), would not be subject to this kind of objection? Any representation for a human audience will have to be, in some sense, an interpretation in human terms, just as any representation of a non-European culture's speech for a European audience would have to be in European terms, in the sense that it will have to try to locate the meaning of the speech in terms of the closest equivalent forms of life.

The problem we run into here is the problem familiar from the case of representing human cultural difference, of translation and indeterminacy. For there are many well-known traps and difficulties in such representation in the human case, and in establishing or assuming equivalence in forms of life in the human case. These ensure that a weak analogue to anthropomorphism is involved in virtually any translation project, in any attempt to 'bring over' one culture's forms into another's. To avoid delegitimating all such attempts, we need to distinguish weaker and stronger forms of anthropomorphism, just as we need to distinguish weak and usually harmless forms of anthropocentrism from strong and damaging forms.[17]

An unwarrantedly or strongly 'Euromorphic' depiction of another culture's customs and speech would involve a methodology which tended unquestioningly to impose a European framework of expectations and norms, failing to note non-equivalences in forms of life or to treat difficulties about translation as sources of uncertainty and tentativeness. On this model, we might expect an appropriate methodology for dealing with difference and translation indeterminacy in the non-human case to be one which could hold relatively open expectations, noting the presence of uncertainty and adopting a tentative stance which explored a range of alternatives and attempted to imagine and situate concept formation in terms of different forms of life. Both human and non-human cases require openness to the other and careful, sensitive, and above all, self-critical observation which admitted and allowed for perspectival and 'centric' biases.[18] The problems in representing another species' speech or subjectivity in human terms are real, but they do not rule out such representation in any general way, and they pale before the difficulties of failing to represent them at all, or before the enormity of representing communicative and intentional beings as beings lacking all communicative and mental capacity. That is a much greater inaccuracy and injustice than any anthropomorphism.

These points show I think that the charge of anthropomorphism cannot be used in a general way to delegitimate representations of non-humans as communicative subjects; charges of strong anthropomorphism may still be viable but require much more work to situate and establish than is usually accorded them. With weak anthropomorphism, the question is not whether or not some degree of humanisation is present in any particular representation of animal communication or of animal characteristics, but how damaging it is, and for what purposes? Undoubtedly there can be great variations and moral differences here, but again, we cannot rule out the mixed perspective which places a human subjectivity into an animal situation, for example, as worthless

---

17   Val Plumwood, 'Androcentrism and anthrocentrism: Parallels and politics', *Ethics and the environment*, Vol. 1 No. 2, 1996, 119–152.
18   Sandra Harding, *Whose science, whose knowledge?* Milton Keynes, Open University Press, 1999.

or unenlightening, especially in a radically non-veridical (fairy tale, fictional or cartoon) context where fidelity is not a virtue. Indeed, as the Larsen cartoon demonstrates, such 'anthropomorphic' transferences of perspective, especially where conscious of their human importations, may be not only funny but philosophically revealing, about ourselves as well as about the other. But if there is no *general* argument that such weakly anthropomorphic mixtures are deceptive and illegitimate, specific cases have to be argued on their merits, not in terms of the alleged intrusion of human impurities but in terms of the kinds of insights they present or prevent and the moral quality of their representation.

Anthrocentrism is a clearer concept than anthropomorphism (although by no means uncontested or unambiguous),[19] and one which also bears more clearly on the moral quality of an artwork that represents the animal. Compare the kind of humanisation displayed in *Babe* with the Disney paradigm of humanisation. Disney cartoons are usually only superficially about animals; Disney characters with stereotypical animal bodies often have totally humanised personalities, frequently incorporate little or no recognisable reference to the characteristics or situations of the animals represented, and permit no representation of their relationship to the human or membership of the mixed community. The animal form appears in this anthrocentric conception as a nullity which is made to bear the burden of meanings which have no connection with the animal's own subjectivity or situation. The Disney paradigm, normalised in television cartoons, is one in which animals are, in John Berger's words, 'totally transformed into human puppets' whose main role is to naturalise various hegemonic forms of the human condition by attributing them to the animal 'kingdom'.[20]

The erasure of animals in the Disney animal cartoon is objectionable in ways that directly reflect its anthrocentrism and its contribution to growing human self-enclosure and incorporation of the other, in this case expressed in the inability to encounter the animal as an independent other who is more than a disguised form of self. These incorporative movements also underlie the highly anthrocentric assumption I criticised above, that an 'animal film' can only be taken seriously to the extent that it is actually about humans. In contrast, a less anthrocentric and belittling treatment would take animals seriously as agents, communicative subjects, bearers of knowledge, and members of the mixed community who are able themselves to observe us and perhaps to reflect critically on their relationships with us. On these sorts of criteria of anthrocentrism in the treatment of the animal other, 'our Babe' comes out rather well.

Criminals, women, animals—all these are bearers of a denied or lessened form of subjecthood, which cannot itself command the position of knower but which

---

19   Val Plumwood, 'Androcentrism and anthrocentrism'.
20   John Berger, *About looking*.

is the object of an arrogant form of knowledge which so stereotypes and denies their difference and their speech that they are obliterated as possible subjects of reciprocal exchange or dialogical encounter. As Foucault notes, to be always under such an arrogating observation is also the fate of the prisoner, and as feminists have pointed out, a feminised subjectivity is one in which the subject internalises such a male gaze. John Berger has claimed that this arrogating conception of the other has now gone so far for animals that the animal proper is now irrecoverable for us as a possible other for encounter and communicative exchange. He writes, '... animals are always the observed. The fact that they can observe us has lost all significance. They are the objects of our ever-extending knowledge. What we know about them is an index of our power, and thus an index of what separates us from them. The more we know, the further away they are'.[21] This diagnosis is acute but, in my view, a trifle too fatalistic. Works of art like *Babe* can help us subvert these anthrocentric conceptions of the animal and recover the animal as subject and reciprocal observer rather than as background, passively observed object; thus, in the final shot of *Babe*, it is the animal who looks back.

Meat and the Colonising Contract

Among the film's other pleasures are the way the lead character Babe, from his position as speaking meat, systematically disrupts each of the background assumptions of meat I identified in Part 1. In the initial scenes of the film, we have (briefly) to confront the first assumption of radical discontinuity in the animal gulag, and the second as we are introduced to the meat as a speaking subject. The third assumption, that of a neat, rational and unproblematic hierarchy of considerability based on intellectual ranking, is systematically disrupted by Babe and several other characters throughout the film, and this is one of its main 'breaking out' arising in post-colonial theory themes and best subversive achievements. Thus Babe's assertion of intelligence and communicative status disrupts Fly's comfortable assurances to her puppies that 'only stupid animals' are eaten. This disruption poses ethical and political questions, analogous to questions arising in post-colonial theory about the role of colonial hierarchies, about the distinction between meat and non-meat animals, and about the nature of the human contract with that special, more privileged group of animals who can never be 'meat'.

'Babe' is the name of an innocent, an original, Christ-like pure soul, to whom the first news of the dirty secret of meat is eventually revealed in the outhouse by the revolutionary duck Ferdie—where the meat comes from, where 'babe' ('babies) himself comes from, in an act of disillusionment which neatly parallels that of

---

21   John Berger, *About looking*, p. 16.

the human child newly discovering reproductive and sexual relationships. ('Not the Boss!' breathes the incredulous Babe, in parallel with the child's shocked 'Not my parents!') But it is from the malevolent cat that Babe finally learns the full hurt of the dreadful secret the factory farm and the sinister farm meat household. The unspeakable is finally spoken: pigs are meat, pigs are subjects, and pigs suffer the reductive violence which denies, distances from, and hides their subjectivity. Babe is only called 'pig' while he is alive, but *they use a different word, "pork or bacon", after you are dead'*, explains the satisfied cat, revelling in her privileged, protected status. As Babe's innocence is stripped away bit by bit, we see the gradual unveiling of various levels and kinds of animal oppressions and colonisations—the baring of the 'world of wounds' we all somehow learn to come to terms with as part of our loss of innocence and 'adult' accommodation to an oppressive world.

Positioned as counter to these various unveilings of oppression are various emancipatory comments and viewpoints from the animals who are presented as sceptical and critical spectators of the human show. Their comments deftly expose the politics of the mixed community, especially its human violence and surrogate dog violence, and the strangeness of human ways. They give us positive perspectives on the importance of listening to and being open to others, and on the injustice, distortion and violence of the exclusionary boundaries which keep Babe positioned as meat. We feel the thrill of broken chains, the excitement of emancipation as Babe is gradually enabled to break the boundaries which keep him positioned as meat, finally crossing the privileged threshold of the house from which he has been so pointedly excluded to watch television with the farmer and his surrogate dog–mother Fly.

What I found particularly illuminating here was the exposure of the levels of hierarchy among animals created by human colonisation in the small human empire of the farm, an empire which makes concrete human desire and human will in its social relations and its rational design of the earth and of the animals themselves. The film displays the key role of these boundaries of exclusion and levels of hierarchy *among animals* in maintaining the practices of meat and the non-subject status of the meat animal. The dogs, in the canine equivalent of human chauvinism, attribute their privilege with some complacency to their greater intelligence, but that facile fabrication is disrupted for us nicely by Babe's pig intelligence in some of the film's earliest scenes. What is exposed as unstable, duplicitous and oppressive here is the conventional boundary and contract on which the relatively privileged status of the pet and 'house' animal is based, which bears on the privileged status of dogs and cats in Western society.

Because it reveals the conventionality and instability of the considerability hierarchy among animals, the film provides us with the materials to reconstruct the Contract or political origin story for the privileged group of 'pets' or conventional companion animals. In early times, hunting, farming and shepherding man ('the Boss') in certain societies made a contract with certain wolves: the contract was that they would be given a respected role and position very different from that of other animals, that *they would never be meat*, in return for help with a critical task. That task was their active help in the oppression and imprisonment of other animals, whom they would help confine and construct as meat. *In return for their help in constructing other animals as meat, not only would they themselves never be meat, they would be 'looked after', given a share of the meat themselves.* Their subjectivity would be recognised, and the reductive Cartesian conception would never apply to them. In the same sense as in various human mythic Contracts or founding political stories of alleged mutual benefit, this was a Contract of complicity in meat. But as the disruptions of *Babe* neatly demonstrate, inclusion in the contract class has nothing to do with 'intelligence', and everything to do with complicity.

This contract, originally a contract of privilege in return for complicity in the practice of meat and the domination or elimination of the non-contract animals, is later extended to *the privileged companion animals*—the pets—with which so many of us continue to share our lives, and whom we continue to feed on the flesh of other 'meat' animals. The malevolent cat in *Babe* is seen thus profiting from the death of the Christmas duck, Rosalyn; in real life, non-privileged animals assigned to the 'meat' side of the hierarchy die to make meat for the pets of people who think of themselves unproblematically as animal lovers—kangaroos, dolphins, penguins, anonymous and rare marine animals in yearly billions are slaughtered at some remove to feed the cats and dogs whose own deaths as meat would be unthinkable to their owners. The companion contract, albeit in a form less oriented to the working animal, remains as strong as ever, and is a major factor in constructing our cuddly versus non-cuddly boundary, and our domestic/wild, clean/dirty, house/outside boundaries as well.

For most urban dwellers, which increasingly is most of us, animals of the Contract Class represent our main contact with the animal world. This is unfortunate, because the Companion Contract reflects and repeats many of the duplicities, denials and exclusions involved in the surrounding Western institution of meat. In historical terms, it is the equivalent of the key colonial contract of empire, the one the coloniser has always been able to make, to his great advantage, with the privileged class among the colonised. In the history of the colonisation of Scotland and Ireland, and everywhere in the history of colonisation, some privileged class of the indigenous is selected to carry out the coloniser's dirty work and to control and oppress indigenous populations.

Without this type of contract, colonisation, in most cases, would not have been possible. This type of contract depends on erecting dualistic boundaries, originally based on instrumental criteria of merit as cooperativeness, complicity and assimilation, and on the need to use some of the colonised to exploit and imprison others. This contract creates the strongly dualistic boundaries of the 'pet' and 'meat' animal; the pet animal is a communicative and ethical subject, ideally subject to consideration, the meat animal is not. The contract forms part of an assimilationist strategy toward the other, in which they are recognised by the colonising self just to the extent that they resemble, express or serve the Self. It is this tainted division that enables our simultaneous claim to love some animals and to have a right to ruthlessly exploit other animals who are not very different, to simultaneously admit pet subjectivity and ignore or deny meat–animal subjectivity.

The contract does much to explain the extraordinary contradictions involved in our contemporary treatment of animals and our claims to love and respect animals. For example, it is this original colonising contract that 'animal lovers' honour when they, perhaps even sometimes as vegetarians or vegans themselves, bring into existence and even breed pet animals whom they feed on the 'meat' of other animals; or whom pet lovers irresponsibly introduce to inappropriate environments where they are permitted to make other animals meat and to disrupt carefully balanced and negotiated communities of free-living animals. These result in such abuses as the dumping of domestic cats in the wild by 'animal lovers', to become a menace to indigenous animals in contexts like Australia where there may be few checks and balances.

It is essential to break down this residual contract and its associated dualisms if we are to overcome the taboo against recognising the subjectivity of the meat animal, as well as the general failure to recognise animal subjectivity. The moral dualism of this contract plays a key role in obscuring the immorality of meat, especially factory farmed meat. Most people have had some positive experiences with such animals as dogs or cats, have allowed themselves to experience them as narrative and communicative subjects rather than as Cartesian 'machine–animals' or as mindless bodies. But it is the ethical dualism and impermeability of this contract boundary which prevents them transferring this awareness to other animals considered 'meat animals' or to wild animals, and which is reflected in the contradiction of the animal lover's horror taboo against eating dogs and contrasting indifference or complacency about the horrific treatment of the 'meat animal'.

Babe takes us quite some distance then towards pushing over this key barrier to a better consciousness of the moral status of all animals, showing us how Babe is excluded from the contract as meat, and how both Babe and the sheep are oppressed by the privileged status of the dogs and cats. But in another crucial way the film fails to resolve some key issues surrounding the contract. For one way to read Babe's liberation in the end of the film is as the supposition that the colonising contract can and should be extended, that Babe's liberation consists in joining or displacing the dogs in the colonising contract, now recast in the role of non-violent communicator with the rest of the farm animals.

Is Babe's liberation then no more than that of the pet, the correction of a mistaken individual placement in the hierarchical order of rational meritocracy? Or can Babe's liberation be somehow extended to all other animals? Here we come up against the liberal understanding of liberation as individual salvation, which generates the same problems that various human liberation movements encounter in liberalism. To the extent that it is an exclusionary contract, in which some make a living by complicity in instrumentalising, imprisoning and oppressing others, the contract of colonisation cannot be extended to provide liberation for all. Such a contract cannot be made liberatory for all by being extended to each, one at a time, and the attempt to do so merely re-erects the moral dualist barrier in a new place.

If Babe is to be saved because of his resemblance to the human and his discontinuity from other animals, we can recognise this as the same colonising contract some forms of liberal feminism have endorsed, to elevate some by complicity in the oppression of others. Feminists such as Elizabeth Cady Stanton, for example, argued that women should be admitted to the privileged class of political rights-holders in virtue of their discontinuity with allegedly 'lower groups' such as negro slaves, and their similarity to the master group, elite white men. The door opens to admit a few, but closes to keep the rest outside where they were. One boundary of moral dualism is momentarily penetrated, but the rest remain in place or new ones are constructed. So the film apparently displays Babe's liberation, but leaves us with the big questions about whether Babe will be admitted alone, with all other pigs, with some other pigs, with all other animals, or with everything we might consider food? That the political vision of animal liberation poses many of the same political and recognition problems and ambiguities that appear for human liberation should be no surprise. It is yet another confirmation of our kinship.

Third section

6. Animals and ecology: Towards a better integration

'Agriculture has become agribusiness after all. So the creatures that have been under our "stewardship" the longest, that have been codified by habit for our use, that have always suffered a special place in our regard—the farm animals—have never been as cruelly kept or confined or slaughtered in such numbers in all of human history. ... The factory farm today is a crowded stinking bedlam, filled with suffering animals that are quite literally insane, sprayed with pesticides and fattened on a diet of growth stimulants, antibiotics, and drugs. Two hundred and fifty thousand laying hens are confined within a single building. (The high mortality rate caused by overcrowding is economically acceptable; nothing is more worthless than an individual chicken).' (Williams 1997)

Ecological animalism versus ontological veganism

Many thinking people have come to believe that there is something profoundly wrong in commodity culture's relationship to living things. That something is expressed perhaps most obviously in the factory farms that profit from distorting and instrumentalising animal lives. In numerous books and articles I have argued that these abuses are enabled and justified by a dominant human-centred ideology of mastery over an inferior sphere of animals and nature.[1] It is this ideology that is expressed in economies that treat commodity animals reductively as less than they are, as a mere human resource, little more than living meat or egg production units.

People aiming to clarify and deepen their experience of contemporary abuse of animals and nature face an important set of choices in philosophical theory. In particular, they have to choose whether to opt for theories of animal ethics and ontology that emphasise discontinuity and set human life apart from animals and ecology, or theories that emphasise human continuity with other life forms and situate both human and animal life within an ethically and ecologically conceived universe. I represent this choice in this paper by comparing two

---

1   See especially, Plumwood, *Feminism and the mastery of nature*, London, Routledge, 1993; 'Integrating ethical frameworks for animals, humans and nature: A critical feminist eco-socialist analysis', *Ethics and the environment*, Vol. 5 No. 3, 2000, pp. 1–38; *Environmental culture: The ecological crisis of reason*, London, Routledge, 2002.

theories that challenge—in quite different ways—the dominant ideology of mastery. Ontological Veganism is a theory that advocates universal abstention from all use of animals as the only real alternative to mastery and the leading means of defending animals against its wrongs. But, I shall argue, another theory which also supports animal defence which I shall call Ecological Animalism, more thoroughly disrupts the ideology of mastery, and is significantly better than Ontological Veganism for environmental awareness, for human liberation, and for animal activism itself.

Ecological Animalism supports and celebrates animals and encourages a dialogical ethics of sharing and negotiation or partnership between humans and animals, while undertaking a re-evaluation of human identity that affirms inclusion in animal and ecological spheres. The theory I shall develop is a context-sensitive semi-vegetarian position, which advocates great reductions in first-world meat-eating and opposes reductive and disrespectful conceptions and treatments of animals, especially in factory farming. The dominant human mastery position that is deeply entrenched in Western culture has constructed a great gulf or dualism between humans and nature, which I call human/nature dualism. Human/nature dualism conceives humans as inside culture but 'outside nature', and conceives non-humans as outside ethics and culture. The theory I advocate aims to disrupt this deep historical dualism by re-situating humans in ecological terms at the same time as it re-situates non-humans in ethical and cultural terms. It affirms an ecological universe of mutual use, and sees humans and animals as mutually available for respectful use in conditions of equality. Ecological Animalism uses the philosophical method of contextualising to allow us to express our care for both animals and ecology, and to acknowledge at the same time different cultures in different ecological contexts, differing nutritional situations and needs, and multiple forms of oppression.

The theory I shall recommend rejecting, Ontological Veganism, has numerous problems for both theory and activism on animal equality and ecology. It ties strategy, philosophy and personal commitment tightly to personal veganism, abstention from eating and using animals as a form of individual action. Ontological Veganism insists that neither humans or animals should ever be conceived as edible or even as usable, confirming the treatment of humans as 'outside nature' that is part of human/nature dualism, and blocking any re-conception of animals and humans in fully ecological terms. Because it is indiscriminate in proscribing all forms of animal use as having the same moral status, it fails to provide philosophical guidance for animal activism that would prioritise action on factory farming over less abusive forms of farming. Its universalism makes it highly ethnocentric, universalising a privileged 'consumer' perspective, ignoring contexts other than contemporary Western urban ones, or aiming to treat them as minor, deviant 'exceptions' to what it takes to be the ideal or norm. Although it claims to oppose the dominant mastery position, it remains subtly human-centred because it does not fully challenge human/nature dualism, but rather attempts to extend human status and privilege to a bigger class of 'semi-humans' who, like humans themselves, are conceived as above the non-conscious sphere and 'outside nature', beyond ecology and beyond use, especially use in the food chain. In doing so it stays within the system of human/nature dualism and denial that prevents the dominant culture from recognising its ecological embeddedness and places it increasingly at ecological risk.

Human/nature dualism is a Western-based cultural formation going back thousands of years that sees the essentially human as part of a radically separate order of reason, mind, or consciousness, set apart from the lower order that comprises the body, the animal and the pre-human. Inferior orders of humanity, such as women, slaves and ethnic Others ('barbarians'), partake of this lower sphere to a greater degree, through their supposedly lesser participation in reason and greater participation in lower 'animal' elements such as embodiment and emotionality. Human/nature dualism conceives the human as not only superior to but as different in kind from the non-human, which as a lower sphere exists as a mere resource for the higher human one. This ideology has been functional for Western culture in enabling it to exploit nature with less constraint, but it also creates dangerous illusions in denying embeddedness in and dependency on nature, which we see in our denial of human inclusion in the food web and in our response to the ecological crisis.

Human/nature dualism is a double-sided affair, destroying the bridge between the human and the non-human from both ends, as it were, for just as the essentially human is disembodied, disembedded and discontinuous from the rest of nature, so nature and animals are seen as mindless bodies, excluded from the realms of ethics and culture. Re-envisaging ourselves as ecologically embodied beings akin to rather than superior to other animals is a major challenge for Western culture, as is recognising the elements of mind and culture present in animals and the non-human world. The double-sided character of human/nature dualism gives rise to two tasks which must be integrated. These are the tasks of situating human life in ecological terms and situating non-human life in ethical terms. Ecological Animalism takes up both of these tasks, whereas Ontological Veganism addresses only the second.

Conventional animalist and conventional ecological theories as they have evolved in the last four decades have each challenged only one side of this double dualist dynamic, and they have each challenged different sides, with the result that they have developed in highly conflictual and incompatible ways. Although each project has a kind of egalitarianism between the human and non-human in mind, their partial analyses place them on a collision course. *The ecology movement has been situating humans as animals, embodied inside ecological systems of mutual use, of food and energy exchange, just as the animal defence movement has been trying to expand an extension to animals of the (dualistic) human privilege of being conceived as outside these systems.* Many animal defence activists seem to believe that ecology can be ignored and that talk of the food web is an invention of hamburger companies, while the ecological side often retains the human-centred resource view of animals and scientist resistance to seeing animals as individuals with life stories of attachment, struggle and tragedy not unlike our own, refusing to apply ethical thinking to the non-human sphere. As I will show, a more double-sided understanding of and challenge to human/nature dualism can help us move on towards a synthesis, a more integrated and less conflictual theory of animals and ecology, if not yet a unified one.

Non-use or respectful use?

Human/nature dualism constructs a polarised set of alternatives in which the idea that humans are above embodiment and thus any form of bodily use is complemented at the opposite extreme by the idea that non-humans are only bodies and are totally instrumentalisable, forming a contrast based on radical exclusion. Human/animal discontinuity is constructed in part by denying overlap and continuity between humans and animals, especially in relation to food: non-human animals can be our food, but we can never be their food. Factory farmed animals are conceived as reducible to food, whereas humans are beyond this and can never be food. Domination emerges in the pattern of usage in which humans are users who can never themselves be used, and which constructs commodity animals in highly reductionist terms.

Although, by definition, all ecologically embodied beings exist as food for some other beings, the human supremacist culture of the West makes a strong effort to deny human ecological embodiment by denying that we humans can be positioned in the food chain in the same way as other animals. Predators of humans have been execrated and largely eliminated. This denial that we ourselves are food for others is reflected in many aspects of our death and burial practices—the strong coffin, conventionally buried well below the level of soil fauna activity, and the slab over the grave to prevent anything digging us up, keeps the Western human body (at least sufficiently affluent ones) from becoming food for other species. Sanctity is interpreted as guarding ourselves jealously and keeping ourselves apart, refusing even to conceptualise ourselves as edible, and resisting giving something back, even to the worms and the land that nurtured us. Horror movies and stories reflect this deep-seated dread of becoming food for other forms of life: horror is the wormy corpse, vampires sucking blood and sci-fi monsters trying to eat humans (*Alien* 1 and 2). Horror and outrage usually greet stories of other species eating live or dead humans, and various levels of hysteria our nibbling by leeches, sandflies, and mosquitoes.

Upon death the human essence is seen as departing for a disembodied, non-earthly realm, rather than nurturing those earth others who have nurtured us. This concept of human identity positions humans outside and above the food web, not as part of the feast in a chain of reciprocity but as external manipulators and masters separate from it. Death becomes a site for apartness, domination and individual salvation, rather than for sharing and for nurturing a community of life. Being food for other animals shakes our image of human mastery. As eaters of others who can never ourselves be eaten in turn by them or even conceive ourselves in edible terms, we take, but do not give, justifying this one way arrangement by the traditional Western view of human rights to use earth others as validated by an order of rational meritocracy in which humans emerge on top. Humans are not even to be conceptualised as edible, not only by other humans, but by other species.

But humans *are* food, food for sharks, lions, tigers, bears and crocodiles, food for crows, snakes, vultures, pigs, rats and goannas, and for a huge variety of smaller creatures and micro-organisms. An Ecological Animalism would acknowledge this and affirm principles emphasising human–animal mutuality, equality and reciprocity in the food web; all living creatures are food, and also much more than food. *In a good human life we must gain our food in such a way as to acknowledge our kinship with those whom we make our food, which does not forget the more than food that every one of us is, and which positions us reciprocally as food for others.* This kind of account does not need to erect a moral dualism or rigid hierarchy to decide which beings are beneath moral consideration and are thus available to be ontologised as edible, and does not need to treat non-animal life as lesser. Its stance of respect and gratitude provides a strong basis for opposing factory farming and for minimising the use of sensitive beings for food.

A more egalitarian vision of ecological embodiment as involving not apartness but mutual and respectful use has been articulated by many ecological thinkers and Indigenous philosophies. Thus Francis Cook, elaborating the ecological philosophy of Hua–Yen Buddhism, writes:

> I depend upon [other] things in a number of ways, one of which is to use them for my own benefit. For I could not exist for a day if I could not use them. Therefore, in a world in which I must destroy and consume in order to continue to exist, I must use what is necessary with gratitude and respect … I must be prepared to accept that I am made for the use of the other no less than it is made for my use … that this is the tiger's world as well as mine, and I am for the use of hungry tigers as much as carrots are for my use.[2]

---

2   Francis Cook, Hua–Yen *Buddhism: The jewel net of Indra*, Philadelphia, Pennsylvania University Press, 1977.

A corollary of accepting that one is for the use of the other is willingness to share one's region with predators of humans and to support the restoration to their original range of the many endangered species of large animals whom human dominance is eliminating from the face of the earth.

Ontological Veganism's treatment of use and instrumentalism could hardly be a greater contrast; it extends vegetarianism, prohibiting animal use as food, to veganism, prohibiting any kind of use. For Ontological Vegans all the problems of animal reduction, of denial of animal communicativity, individuality and basic needs in factory farming stem from a simple cause—ontologising them as edible. It is a curious and paradoxical feature of Ontological Veganism that it basically shares the taboo on envisaging the human in edible terms, and that its strategy for greater equality is the extensionist one of attempting to extend this taboo to a wider class of beings. The paradox is that it was precisely in order to give expression to such a radical separation between humans and other animals that the taboo on conceiving humans as edible was developed in the first place.

Carol Adams in various books and articles[3] provides a very useful and thorough account of the commodity concept of meat as a reductionist form and of associated food concepts and practices as sites of domination. However, Adams goes on to present the reductions and degradations of animals she describes so convincingly as the outcome of ontologising them as edible.[4] But saying that seeing earth others as edible is responsible for their degraded treatment as 'meat' is much like saying that ontologising human others as sexual beings is responsible for rape or sexual abuse. Ontologising others as sexual beings is not correctly identified as the salient condition for rape or sexual abuse; rather it is the identification of sexuality with domination. Similarly, it is the identification of food practices with human domination and mastery that underlies the abusive use of food animals. The complete exclusion of use denies ecological embodiment and the important alternative of respectful use.

Thus Carol Adams argues that any use of the animal other (for food or anything else) involves instrumentalising them,[5] stating that, 'the ontologising of animals as edible bodies creates them as instruments of human beings'.[6] Instrumentalism is widely recognised (although often unclearly conceptualised) as a feature of oppressive conceptual frameworks, but instrumentalism is mis-defined by Adams as involving any making use of the other, rather than reductive treatment of the other as *no more than* something of use, a means to an end. This

---

3   Carol Adams, *The sexual politics of meat: A feminist–vegetarian critical theory*, New York, Continuum, 1990; 'The feminist traffic in animals', in Greta Gaard, ed. *Ecofeminism: Women, animals and nature*, Philadelphia, Temple University Press, 1993; *Neither man nor beast: Feminism and the defense of animals*, New York, Continuum, 1994.
4   Carol Adams, 'The feminist traffic in animals', p. 103.
5   Carol Adams, 'The feminist traffic in animals', p. 200.
6   Carol Adams, *Neither man nor beast*, p. 103.

definition of instrumentalism as the same as use is not a viable way to define instrumentalism even in the human case—since there are many cases where we can make use of one another for a variety of purposes without incurring any damaging charge of instrumentalism.[7] The circus performers who stand on one another's shoulders to reach the trapeze are not involved in any oppressively instrumental practices. Neither is someone who collects animal droppings to improve a vegetable garden. In both cases the other is used, but is also seen as more than something to be used, and hence not treated instrumentally. Rather instrumentalism has to be understood as involving a reductionist conception in which the other is subject to disrespectful or totalising forms of use and defined as no more than a means to some set of ends.

Discontinuity, culture and nature: Demonising and exceptionalising predation

By affirming that we ourselves are subject to use and that all uses of others must involve respect for individual and species life, an Ecological Animalism can affirm continuity of life-forms, including humans. An Ontological Veganism that occludes the possibility of respectful use and treats food as degraded must assume that only things that are not morally considerable can be eaten. It is then tied to an exclusionary imperative, requiring a cut-off point to delineate a class beneath ethical consideration, on pain of having nothing left to eat. Such positions retain the radical discontinuity of Cartesian dualism, repositioning the boundary of ethical consideration at a different point (higher animals possessing 'consciousness'), but still insisting on an outsider class of sensitive living creatures virtually reduced to machine status and conceived as 'beyond ethics'. It is a paradox that, although it claims to increase our sensitivity and ethical responsiveness to the extended class of almost-humans, such a position also serves to reduce our sensitivity to the vast majority of living organisms which remain in the excluded class beyond consideration.

Ontological Veganism's subtle endorsement of human/nature dualism and discontinuity also emerges in its treatment of predation and its account of the nature/culture relationship. Predation is often demonised as bringing unnecessary pain and suffering to an otherwise peaceful vegan world of female gathering, and in the human case is seen as an instrumental male practice of domination directed at animals and women. But if instrumentalism is not the same as simply making use of something, and even less thinking of making use of it (ontologising it as edible), predation is not necessarily an instrumental practice, especially if it finds effective ways to recognise that the other is more

---

7   On Kant's basically confused treatment of this problem see my discussion in Plumwood, 1993, chapter 6.

than 'meat'. Ecologically, predation is presented as an unfortunate exception and animals, like women, as always victims: fewer than 20% of animals, Adams tells us, are predators[8]—a claim that again draws on a strong discontinuity between plants and animals. In this way it is suggested that predation is unnatural and fundamentally eliminable. But percentage tallies of carnivorous species are no guide to the importance of predation in an ecosystem or its potential eliminability.

An Ecological Animalist could say that it is not predation as such that is the problem but what certain social systems make of predation. Thus I would agree that hunting is a harmful, unnecessary and highly gendered practice within some social contexts, but reject any general demonisation of hunting or predation, which would raise serious problems about Indigenous cultures and about flow-on from humans to animals. Any attempt to condemn predation in general, ontological terms will inevitably rub off onto predatory animals (including both carnivorous and omnivorous animals), and any attempt to separate predation completely from human identity will also serve to reinforce once again the Western tradition's hyper-separation of our nature from that of animals, and its treatment of Indigenous cultures as animal-like. This is another paradox, since it is one of the aims of the vegan theory to affirm our kinship and solidarity with animals, but here its demonisation of predation has the opposite effect, of implying that the world would be a better place without predatory animals. Ontological Vegans hope to avoid this paradox, but their attempts to do so, I shall argue, are unsuccessful and reveal clearly that their worldview rests on a dualistic account of human identity.

The main move Ontological Vegans make to minimise the significance of predation and block the problematic transfer of their anti-predation stance from humans to animals is to argue that human predation is situated in culture while animal predation is situated in nature.[9] Human participation in predation therefore cannot be justified as participation in an integral natural process, as philosophers like Holmes Rolston have justified it. Against simple naturalism, Moriarty and Woods argue that 'meat eating and hunting are cultural activities, not natural activities'.[10] They claim that 'our distinctively human evolutionary achievement—culture—has strongly separated us from non-human nature. We have found freedom from ecosystems ... [and] are no longer a part of ecosystems'. Because meat-eating is influenced by culture it can be considered to 'involve no participation in the logic and biology of natural ecosystems'.[11] For Ontological Vegans, human hunting and meat-eating has an entirely different status from the 'instinctual' predatory activity of non-human animals—so much so that they treat the term 'predation' as inadmissible for the case of human hunting.

---

8 Carol Adams, 'The feminist traffic in animals', p. 200.
9 Carol Adams, 'The feminist traffic in animals', p. 399; Paul Veatch Moriarty & Mark Woods, 'Hunting ≠ Predation', *Environmental ethics*, Vol. 19 Winter, 1997.
10 Moriarty & Woods, p. 399.
11 Ibid, p. 401.

There are several further problems and paradoxes here. One paradox is that animal activists who have stressed our continuity with and similarity with animals in order to ground our obligation to extend ethics to them now stress their complete dissimilarity and membership of a separate order, as inhabitants of nature not culture, in order to avoid a flow-on to animals of demonising predation. Embracing the claim that humans 'don't live in nature' in order to block the disquieting and problem-creating parallel between human hunting and animal predation introduces a cure which is worse than the disease and which is basically incompatible with any form of ecological consciousness. The claim that humans are not a part of natural ecosystems is on a collision course with most fundamental points of ecological understanding because it denies the fundamental ecological insight that human culture is embedded in ecological systems and dependent on nature. It also denies an important insight many students of animals have rightly stressed—that culture, learning and choice is not unique to the human and that non-human animals also have culture. In fact Woods and Moriarty's solution rests on a thoroughly dualistic and hyper-separated understanding of human identity and of the terms 'nature' and 'culture'. In order to attain the desired human–animal separation, nature must be 'pure' nature, 'strictly biological', and culture conceived as 'pure' culture, no longer in or of nature: an activity is no longer natural if it shows any cultural influence, and culture is completely disembedded from nature, 'held aloft on a cloud in the air'.

Of course Ontological Vegans are right to object to any simple naturalisation of human hunting and meat eating. On the kind of account I have given, both the claim that meat eating is in nature rather than culture and the counter-claim that it is in culture and therefore not in nature are wrong and are the product of indefensible hyper-separated ways of conceptualising both these categories that are characteristic of human/nature dualism. It is only if we employ these hyper-separated senses that the distinction between nature and culture can be used to block the flow-on problem that demonising human predation also demonises animal predation. On the sort of account I have given above, any form of human eating (and many forms of non-human eating) is situated in both nature and culture—in nature as a biologically necessary determinable and in a specific culture as a determinate form subject to individual and social choice and practice. Food, like most other human (and many non-human activities) is a thoroughly mixed activity, not one somehow throwing together bits of two separate realms, but one expressing through the logic of the determinate–determinable relationship one aspect of the 'intricate texture' of the embedment of culture in nature. Both naturalising and culturalising conceptual schemes are inadequate to deal with the problem, both sides of this debate deny the way our lives weave together and criss-cross narratives of culture and nature, and the way our food choices are shaped and constrained both by our social and by our ecological context.

Universalism and ethnocentrism

Ontological Veganism assumes a universalism which is ethnocentric and fails to allow adequately for cultural diversity and for alternatives to consumer culture. Carol Adams' work, for example, follows a methodology that universalises a US consumer perspective and hopes to deal with other cultures as exceptions to the 'general' rule. Universalism is supplemented by an exceptionalist methodology which dispenses excuses for those too frail to follow its absolute abstentionist prescriptions. Deviations from the norm or ideal 'may occur at rare times', when justified by necessity.[12] A methodology which deals with universal human activities such as eating in terms of US-centred cultural assumptions applicable at most to the privileged 20%, treating the bulk of the world's people as 'deviations' or exceptions, is plainly highly ethnocentric.

In addition, Adams strives to assimilate all possible animal food practices to those of commodity culture in what seems to be an effort to deny that any cultural difference involving non-instrumental forms of eating animals can exist. Thus her discussion of the cultural context of the 'relational hunt' (a crude attempt to model non-instrumental Indigenous food practices) criticises those who refuse to absolutise the vegan imperative, declaring that 'there is, in general, no need to be eating animals'.[13] She goes on to suggest that eating an animal after a successful hunt, like cannibalism in emergency situations, is sometimes necessary, but like cannibalism is morally repugnant, and should properly be marked by disgust. Clearly Indigenous foraging cultures are among those that would fall far short of such an ideal.

Ontological Veganism is based around a mythical gender anthropology which valorises Western women's alleged 'gathering' roles in contrast to demonic 'male' hunting. A cultural hegemony that falsifies the lives of Indigenous men and women underlies the strong opposition it assumes between 'male hunting' and 'female gathering', the sweeping assumption that 'women' do not hunt and that female-led 'gathering' societies were vegetarian or plant-based.[14] The assumption is that active, aggressive men hunt large animals in what is envisaged as a precursor of warfare, while passive, peaceful women gather or nurture plants in a precursor of agriculture. This imaginary schema reads contemporary Western meanings of gender and hunting back in a universal way into other cultures, times and places, assuming a gendered dualism of foraging activities

---

12 Carol Adams, 'Neither man nor beast', p. 103.
13 Ibid.
14 Andree Collard with Joyce Contrucci, *Rape of the wild: man's violence against animals and the earth*, Bloomington, Indiana University Press, 1989; Marti Kheel, 'From heroic to holistic ethics', in Greta Gaard, ed., *Ecofeminism: Women, animals and nature*, and 'Licence to kill: An ecofeminist critique of hunters' discourse', in Adams & Donovan, eds., *Animals and women*, Duke University Press, 1995; Carol Adams, 'Comments on George's "Should feminists be vegetarians?"', *Signs*, Autumn 1995, pp. 221–229.

in which the mixed forms encountered in many Indigenous societies are denied and disappeared. Thus Adams urges us to base our alternative ideals not on hunting societies but on 'gatherer societies that demonstrate humans can live well without depending on animals' bodies as food'.[15] But no such purely vegan 'gatherer' societies have ever been recorded! Adams denies the undeniable evidence from contemporary Indigenous women's foraging practices that they often include far more than collecting plants. Australian Aboriginal women's gathering contributes as much as 80% of tribal food, but women's 'gathering' has always involved killing a large variety of small to medium animals. This is not a matter of speculation about the past, but of well-confirmed present-day observation and Indigenous experience.

In assuming that alternatives to animal food are always or 'generally' available Adams universalises a context of consumer choice and availability of alternatives to animal food which ignores the construction of the lifeways of well-adapted Indigenous cultures around the ecological constraints of their country, which do not therefore represent inessential features of ethnic cultures in the way she assumes.[16] The successful human occupation of many places and ecological situations in the world has required the use of at least some of their animals for food and other purposes: the most obvious examples here are places like the high Arctic regions, where for much of the year few vegetable resources are available, but other Indigenous 'gathering–hunting' cultures are similarly placed—for example Australian Aboriginal cultures, whose survival in harsh environments relies on the finely detailed knowledge and skilful exploitation of a very wide variety of seasonally available foods of all kinds, essential among which may be many highly valued animal foods gathered by women and children.

This gives rise to another paradox: the superficially sensitive Ontological Vegan can implicitly assume an insensitive and ecologically destructive economic context. From the perspective of the 'biosphere person' who draws on the whole planet for nutritional needs defined in the context of consumer choices in the global market, it is relatively easy to be a vegan and animal food is an unnecessary evil. But the lifestyle of the biosphere person is, in the main, destructive and ecologically unaccountable. From the perspective of the more ecologically accountable 'ecosystem person' who must provide for nutritional needs from within a small, localised group of ecosystems, however, it is very difficult or impossible to be vegan: in the highly constrained choice context of the ecosystem person some animal-based foods are indispensable to survival.

---

15   Carol Adams, 'Neither man nor beast', p. 105.
16   On the construction of Australian Indigenous cultures around their ecological contexts see Deborah Bird Rose, *Nourishing terrains: Australian Aboriginal views of landscape and wilderness*, Canberra, Australian Heritage Commission, 1996.

Vegan approaches to food that rely implicitly upon the global marketplace are thus in conflict with ecological approaches that stress the importance of ecological accountability and of local adaptation.

A similarly ethnocentric and inadequately contextualised methodology is applied by Ontological Vegans to the issue of the ecological consequences of animal food. The cultural hegemony and universalism openly espoused by leading vegan theorists assimilates all planetary meat-eating practices to those of North American grain-feeding and its alternatives, and is insensitive to the culturally variable ecological consequences involved in the use of other animals as food. Animal defence theorists stress the ecological and health benefits of eating lower down the food chain.[17] These principles may be a useful general guide, but they are subject to many local contextual variations that are not recognised by Ontological Vegans. In some contexts, for instance that of the West Australian wheat belt, the ecological costs of land degradation (including costs to non-human animals) associated with grain production are so high that eating free-living, low-impact grazing animals like kangaroos must at least sometimes carry much lower animal and ecological costs than eating vegetarian grains. A vegan diet derived from this context could be in conflict with obligations to eat in the least harmful and ecologically costly way.

Veganism does not necessarily minimise ecological costs and can be in conflict in some contexts with ecological eating. Yet vegan universalists employ a set of simplistic arguments which are designed to show that the vegan way must always and everywhere coincide with the way that is least costly ecologically. David Waller for example cites as decisive and universally applicable statistics drawn from the North American context comparing the ecological costs of meat and grain eating. This comparison is supposed to show grain is ecologically better and dispose of the problem of conflict between animal rights and ecological ethics. But these universalist comparisons assume that grain production for human use is always virtually free of ecological costs or costs to animal life (whereas it is in many arid land contexts highly damaging to the land and to biodiversity). They ignore the fact that in much of the world animals used for food are not grain-fed, and that the rangeland over which they graze is often not suitable for crop tillage agriculture.

Suitability for activism

The appeal of Ontological Veganism largely depends on the false contrast it draws between veganism and commodity culture traditions of animal reduction

---

17   John Robbins, *Diet for a new America*, Walpole, N.H, Stillpoint, 1987; David Waller, 'A vegetarian critique of deep and social ecology' *Ethics and the environment*, Vol. 2 No. 2, 1997, pp. 187–198.

and human/nature dualism, that is between no use at all and ruthless use based on domination and denial. But this is in effect a choice between alienation and domination. Adams' ethnocentric ontological veganism succeeds in this false contrast because its conceptual framework obscures the distinction between meat and animal food, where meat is a determinate cultural construction in terms of domination, and animal food is a cultural determinable. Meat is the result of an instrumentalist–reductionist framework, but the concept of animal food allows us the means to resist the reductions and denials of meat by honouring the edible life form as much more than food, and certainly much more than meat. If we must all, including humans, be ontologised ecologically as edible, as participating in the food web as a condition of our embodiment, that does not mean we must all be ontologised reductively as meat. Food, unlike the reductive category of meat that does not recognise that we are all always more than food, is not a hyper-separated category and does not have to be a disrespectful category.

This distinction enables Ecological Animalism to stand with Ontological Veganism in affirming that no being, human or non-human, should be ontologised reductively as meat, and hence in opposing reductive commoditisation of animals. But unlike Ontological Veganism it can combine the rejection of commoditisation with the framework of ecology and cultural diversity by maintaining that all embodied beings are food and more than food, that is, with an ecological ontology. A careful contextualisation of food practices provides much better guidance for activism than a culturally hegemonic universalism. Ecological Animalism can provide a strong basis for opposing the 'rationalised' commodity farming practices that reduce animals to living meat and are responsible for the great bulk and intensity of domestic animal misery in the modern West. It is of necessity more flexible, less dogmatic and universalist, but can still vindicate the major activist concerns of the animal defence movement. It would require us to avoid complicity in contemporary food practices that abuse animals, especially factory farming, and can agree there are plenty of good reasons for being a vegetarian in modern urban contexts where food sources are untraceable or treatment of animals known to be cruel or reductive. But for Ecological Animalism, vegetarianism would not represent any disgust at 'corpses' or ontological revulsion against our mutual condition as food, but rather protest at the unacceptable conditions of animal life and death in particular societies that reduce animals and commodify their flesh as 'meat', in terms that minimise their claims on us and on the earth. An ecological animalist can affirm the ecological world, despite the fact that it contains predation, necessarily and not only contingently, whereas an Ontological vegetarian is committed to a rejection of the ecological world.

The Ontological Vegan framework in effect presents us with a false choice between no use at all and totally instrumentalising forms of use. By counting all cases of use as instrumentalism, the most considerate and respectful forms of farming which allow animals to lead the kinds of lives they have always led and that are respectful of their species life, amount to the same thing as the worst forms of factory farming in which an animal's entire life is deformed and instrumentalised. By insisting on highly polarised alternatives ('either one eats animals or one does not') Ontological Veganism obscures useful and potentially popular intermediate positions other than the vanguardist position of total abstention, such as semi-vegetarian positions advocating great reductions in the use of animal food and boycotts of those forms of 'meat' that do not respect animal lives or species being. The spaces of ecological ontology and respectful use that are eliminated in Adam's treatment prohibiting any ontologising of others as edible are precisely the ones that could be occupied by alternative models which see the food chain in terms of reciprocity rather than domination or alienation, for example as a sacrament of sharing and exchange of life in which all species ultimately participate as food for others, and the 'moreness' of all beings is recognised.[18]

An over-emphasis on personal conversion and individual abstention has meant a focus on a vanguard politics of individual moral purity. Other forms of popular action based on a politics of coalition and political alliance with other social movements have consequently been under-developed and under-theorised. Recovering a liberatory direction would mean replacing the over-individualised and culturally hegemonic vanguard focus on veganism as a politics of personal virtue and self-denial, with its demonstrated potential for fostering self-righteousness and holier-than-thouism, by a more carefully contextualised vegetarianism, a more diverse and politically sensitive set of strategies for collective action, and by a stronger focus on the responsibility of systems of economic rationality for the atrocities daily committed against animals, especially in the factory–farming framework.

---

18   See Gary Snyder, *The practice of the wild*, New York, North Point Press, 1990. Adams in her discussion of the 'relational hunt' asks in relation to reciprocity, 'what does the animal who dies receive in this exchange' (1994, p. 104). The answer is that it has already received it in life itself, existence as part of the cycle of embodiment and exchange. The idea of the food chain as a cycle of sharing and exchange of life in which all ultimately participate as food for others is what we should understand by reciprocity here.

7. Tasteless: Towards a food-based approach to death

Food/death

Two encounters with death led to my becoming radically dissatisfied with the usual Western selection of death narratives—both Christian–monotheist AND modernist–atheist. I think both major traditions inherit the human exceptionalism and hyper-separation that propels the environmental crisis. However, there are encouraging signs of a developing animist consciousness and mortuary practice that challenges exceptionalism and grasps human death in terms of reciprocity in the earth community.

It has seemed to me since my near-death experience with the crocodile that our worldview denies the most basic feature of animal existence on planet earth— that we are food and that through death we nourish others. As I have written in previous articles, the food/death perspective, so familiar to our ancestors, is something the human exceptionalism of Western modernity has structured out of life. Attention to human foodiness is tasteless. Of course we are all routinely nibbled both during and after life by all sorts of very small creatures, but in the microscopic context our essential foodiness is much easier to ignore than in one where we are munched by a noticeably large predator.

Modernist liberal individualism teaches us that we own our lives and bodies, politically as an enterprise we are running, experientially as a drama we are variously narrating, writing, acting and/or reading. As hyper-individuals, we owe nothing to nobody, not to our mothers, let alone to any nebulous earth community. Exceptionalised as both species and individuals, we humans cannot be positioned in the food chain in the same way as other animals. Predation on humans is monstrous, exceptionalised and subject to extreme retaliation. Dominant concepts of human identity position humans outside and above the food chain, not as part of the feast in a chain of reciprocity. Animals can be our food, but we can never be their food. Human Exceptionalism positions us as the eaters of others who are never themselves eaten and has profoundly shaped dominant practices of self, commodity, materiality and death—especially death. For an ecological culture, major rethinking is required.

The Western problematic of death—where the essential self is disembodied spirit—poses a false choice of continuity, even eternity, in the realm of the spirit, versus the reductive materialist concept of death as the complete ending of the story of the material, embodied self. Both horns of this dilemma exact a terrible price, alienation from the earth in the first case and the loss of meaning and narrative continuity for self in the second.

Indigenous animist concepts of self and death succeed in breaking this pernicious false choice and suggesting satisfying and ecologically responsive forms of continuity with and through the earth. By understanding life as circulation, as a gift from a community of ancestors, we can see death as recycling, a flowing on into an ecological and ancestral community of origins. In place of the Western war of life against death whose battleground has been variously the spirit-identified afterlife and the reduced, medicalised material life, the Indigenous imaginary sees death as part of life, partly through narrative, and partly because death is a return to the (highly narrativised) land that nurtures life. Such a vision of life fosters an imaginary of the land as a nourishing terrain, and of death as a nurturing, material continuity/reunion with ecological others, especially the lives and landforms of country.

My proposal is that the food/death imaginary we have lost touch with is a key to re-imagining ourselves ecologically, as members of a larger earth community of radical equality, mutual nurturance and support. Re-imagining in terms of concrete practices of restraint and humility, not just in vague airy–fairy concepts of unity. Our loss of this perspective has meant the loss of humbling but important forms of knowledge, of ourselves and of our world. We can learn to look for comfort and continuity, meaning and hope in the context of the earth community, and work in this key place to displace the hierarchical and exceptionalist cultural framework that so often defeats our efforts to adapt to the planet.

Atheism, exceptionalism and heavenism

The second experience that disrupted my concepts of death was burying my son in a small country cemetery that was also a refuge for a remarkable botanical community. This experience suggested ways in which a radical animist reconception of identity can re-imagine death in terms of a reciprocity ethic of mutual nurturance.

The exceptionalist denial that we ourselves are food for others is reflected in many aspects of our conventional death and burial practices—the strong coffin, conventionally buried well below the level of soil fauna activity, and the slab over the grave to prevent anything digging us up, supposedly keeps the Western human body from becoming food for other species. The local bush cemetery I found for my son was a place which powerfully enacted the modernist dramas opposing exceptionalist heavenism to exceptionalist–atheism. When I first visited the cemetery on a sunny autumn day, it seemed an extraordinarily serene and beautiful place, a place with a satisfying feeling of the acceptance of mortality. The wounds the old burials had made in the earth had long since healed, and only a few raw scars bore witness to recent ones. But the exceptionalist imaginary that theologian Norman Habel calls 'heavenism' had shaped the old memorials nearest the gate, which date back over a 150 years. From a distance, the tall pillars of marble or sandstone look eerily like pale shrouded forms, already freed from the clay, beginning their journey upwards. Most of these early modern gravestones bore inscriptions invoking a heavenly home, such as, 'Sleep on, dear husband, take they rest/God called you home when he thought it best.' Many inscriptions insist that the earth is an inferior place, best left behind. 'Mourn not for them who God has blest/And taken to their heavenly rest/Freed from all sorrow, grief and pain/Our loss is their eternal gain.'

For heavenism, the earth is at best a temporary lodging; the true human home is beyond the earth, in heaven. Buried six-feet down, the strong wooden or steel coffin aims to keep the heaven-bound body apart from the earth and other life forms for as long as possible and to preserve it for departure to its higher home. For this transcendental solution to the problem of death and continuity, we are split into an embodied and perishable part belonging to earth, and a thinking imperishable 'spirit' part belonging to heaven. Bodies must perish, but the soul, the true self, has eternal life in a realm apart. Such transcendental solutions to the problem of identity and continuity depend on denying our kinship to other life forms and our shared end as food for others. Heavenism is strongly exceptionalist, and its funerary practices deplore or demonise materiality, hyper-separating the human body from the earth and hindering decay that benefits other forms of life. The cemetery itself is exceptionalised as sanctified ground, in contrast to the profane or fallen zone beyond it.

The later (post-1920's) mortuary practices further from the gate express the exceptionalist dynamic in different terms. Gone are the pale standing ghosts, the pointing stone fingers—in their place lies a grey regiment of massive concrete slabs, their rectangles, straight lines and polished surfaces marking the starker vision of modern rationalism and reductive materialism. These memorials are silent about death, the big taboo topic of modernity, and their minimal inscriptions rarely give away more than names and dates. The now-massive slab even more emphatically hyper-separates the human dead from their surroundings and prevents the decaying body from nourishing other forms of life. The expressive poverty of these hyper-expensive memorials represents the silence at the heart of the modernist reductionist paradigm and its concept of death. Their anti-life function is intensified by modern herbicide technology: many slabs are surrounded by large bare areas, where all encroaching vegetation has been poisoned and nothing now can grow.

This lifeless zone is the modernist, concrete expression of the transcendent ideals which continue to hyper-separate human and nature and conceive death as apart from and opposed to life. Its mortuary practice expresses human exceptionalism and the Cartesian project of defeating human mortality not by religion in the afterlife but by a technological–medical war against nature in this life. As I wrote of reductive materialism,[1] 'Contemporary Western identity has rejected the otherworldly significance and basis for continuity, but has given it no other definitive meaning, provided no other satisfactory context for continuity or embeddedness for human life.' Modernity, despite its pride in throwing off the illusions of the past, has failed to provide an ecological or earthian identity or narrative to replace the heavenist one. 'To the extent that death can express an unity (*sic*) with nature, it is a unity with an order of nature conceived as a dualised other, as itself stripped of significance, as mere matter ... death is a nothing, a void, a terrifying and sinister terminus, whose only meaning is that there is no meaning.' The old narratives of post-earth transcendence are dead, but modernity has not replaced them by any meaningful or comforting new ones about earthly life. Hence the modernist avoidance around death these memorials so clearly express.

On this analysis, reductive materialism and associated forms of atheism are not rejection of the heavenist problematic so much as a continuation and even affirmation of it in an amputated form—a reversal in which the original spirit/matter split is maintained but the previously devalued side (the body, materiality) is now affirmed—without however the fuller re-conception of materiality required for a genuine healing of the dualistic problematic. A good deal of contemporary atheism, humanism and materialism expresses only a truncated dualism and disillusioned heavenism, failing to provide alternative reshaping narratives of meaning, comfort and continuity for self and body. (So this kind of materialism is NOT A BOLD NEW BEGINNING, as it usually claims, but is haunted by its lost former half.) What I am arguing here is that an ecological understanding of the self can point towards such reshaping narratives and practices, of which we stand so greatly in need.

It is these conventional dualised choices—spirit or matter—that have framed the central dilemma about death as now conceived in the West: the choice of (narratives of) alienated *continuity* versus reductive–materialist *discontinuity*—the supposed finality of material death, or the narrative of no narratives. On the second, immanent choice of reductive atheism and materialism, the human

---

1   Plumwood, 1993, p. 101.

body is still seen as being peripheral or inessential to identity, so no continuity beyond death can be based on it. Interviewed shortly before her recent death, and openly avowing her atheism, movie star Katherine Hepburn was seen as courageous in her averment that 'death is final' … there is nothing beyond. The death of self (self-lying in individual consciousness) is final and complete. Reductive materialism is marked especially by the Finality Thesis, the claim that death is the final END OF THE STORY. It is this loss of story, the narrative of no narratives, that is expressed in the massive mute modernist headstones.

Animist death: Another story

The thesis of finality shows clearly how both conventional theist and conventional atheist positions collaborate in the conception of matter as a reduced sphere inessential to the self and completely 'left behind' in the ending that death is supposed to represent. Because of course *the body* does not just 'end'—it decays or decomposes, its matter losing its prior organisational form and taking on or being incorporated into new forms in a sharing of substance/life force. Lots of linking, afterlife narratives here!

The finality thesis depends on a covert continuation of the heavenist identification of self with spirit, and on a thoroughly reductionist and denarrativised understanding of the body and of materiality that results from spirit/matter dualism. The finality story subtly accepts the dualist–Cartesian proposition that our essential element is consciousness, so when that finishes, so must 'we.' With the end of consciousness, we are confronted unavoidably with the end of self. A more fluid and embodied concept of self and its boundaries can be employed here to suggest a complex narrative of continuities, in which the story goes on, although no longer mainly a story about human subjects.

There are then important differences in the reductionist versus non-reductionist account of the afterlife. Heavenism expresses exceptionalism in its concept of afterlife in an exclusively human realm utterly apart, while reductionist materialism treats the afterlife in terms of absence, nullity. For an ecological, animist materialism, however, the afterlife is a positive, ecological presence, positive traces in the lives of other species—not no story, but another, continuing story.

The recognition of life as in circulation and of our death as an opportunity for other life can discourage the human greediness and ingratitude that tries to grasp for eternal youth through transcendence, privilege and technological mastery. At the individual level, death confirms transience, but on the level of the ecological community, it can affirm an enduring, resilient cycle or process. Thus the cemetery of my first visit revealed a route to healing grief through the joyful vision it offered of death flowing on into, even a journey into, a tranquil and beautiful landscape. The tranquillity proved illusory, but not the background vision of burial and bodily decay as the ground of entry to a scared ecological community.

Corresponding mortuary symbolisms and grave practices might aim to nourish rather than exclude other life forms, affirming rather than demonising our transition to the non-human in death. It is encouraging to note then in my son's cemetery, the hint of an emerging post-modern mortuary sensibility in the establishment of a lawn cemetery. This at least accepts that living things should grow from a grave. Is the consciousness worm at last starting to turn, with an acceptance of the idea of human recycling beginning to challenge entrenched norms of human apartness represented by the concrete slab?

It is of course not the use of stone itself, even in its subjugated, instrumentalised modern form as the concrete slab, that is the problem, but rather the way stone has been mobilised by our split culture in the service of Human Exceptionalism in an effort to exclude and deny life ('the world of changes' in Plato's terms) and to associate the human essence with an unchanging order of eternity. This use of stone to affirm transcendence of life forgets that we are bodies, plain members of the ecological order, and that our life is a gift from an embodied community of prior others we must nurture. The use of stone to confirm transcendence forgets that stone is the earth's body (or rather skeleton), and like other skeletons, prone to decay. It also forgets the reptiles, for whom stone is generally splendid habitat. On a recent visit to my son's grave to pull out thistles, I was pursued by a tiny, exquisite dragon lizard, flashing its thorny orange mouth in a show of defiance. A gravestone—or even a concrete slab—can make a fine lizard hunting and basking spot, and can easily be redesigned to incorporate a small reptile shelter (let's get the reptiles back into the garden!)

The re-conception of death and the sacred in terms of an animist or ecological materialist imaginary calls, then, for different philosophies, sensibilities and iconographies of death from those normalised in our culture, ones that can revere the burial place as a site of union with the prior sacred presences of earth rather than as set apart from it, and can honour the dissolution of the human into the more-than-human flux. Overcoming the Human Exceptionalism that has had such a deep hold on Western consciousness is the crucial pre-condition for such an animist–materialist spirituality becoming available to us emotionally and culturally.

Works cited

Adams, Carol, 'Ecofeminism and the eating of animals', *Hypatia*, Vol. 6 No. 1, 1991, pp. 125–145.

_____, 'The feminist traffic in animals', in Greta Gaard, ed. *Ecofeminism: Women, animals and nature*, Philadelphia, Temple University Press, 1993.

_____, *The sexual politics of meat*, New York, Continuum, 1994.

_____, *Neither man nor beast: Feminism and the defense of animals*, New York, Continuum, 1994.

_____, 'Comments on George's "Should feminists be vegetarians?"', *Signs*, Autumn 1995, pp. 221–229.

Berger, John, *About Looking*, New York, Vintage, 1991.

Brown, C. Stone, 'Prison guards fund governor for presidential race', *Z Magazine* Sept/October, 1995.

Collard, Andree with Joyce Contrucci, *Rape of the wild: man's violence against animals and the earth*, Bloomington, Indiana University Press, 1989.

Connolly, William E. 'Voices from the whirlwind', in Jane Bennett & William Chaloupka eds. *In the nature of things*, Minneapolis, University of Minnesota Press, 1993.

Cook, Francis, Hua-Yen *Buddhism: The jewel net of Indra*, Philadelphia, Pennsylvania University Press, 1977.

Dryzek, John, *Discursive democracy*, Cambridge, Cambridge University Press, 1990.

Frye, Marilyn, *The politics of reality*, New York, The Crossing Press, 1983.

Harding, Sandra, *Whose science, whose knowledge?* Milton Keynes, Open University Press, 1991.

Harvey, Graham, *Animism: Respecting the living world*, New York, Columbia University Press, 2006.

Hickory, Shagbark, 'Environmental etiquette/environmental practice; American Indian challenges to mainstream environmental ethics', in Max Oelschlaeger ed. *The company of others: Essays in celebration of Paul Shepard*, Durango, Colorado, Kivaki Press, 1995.

Hughes, Robert, *The fatal shore*, Collins, 1987.

Ingold, Tim, *The perception of the environment: Essays in livelihood, dwelling and skill*, London, Routledge, 2000.

Kheel, Marti, 'From heroic to holistic ethics', in Greta Gaard, ed. *Ecofeminism: Women, animals and nature*, Philadelphia, Temple University Press, 1993

Kheel, Marti, 'Licence to kill: An ecofeminist critique of hunters' discourse', in Adams & Donovan, eds. *Animals and women*, Duke University Press, 1995.

King-Smith, Dick, *The Sheep-Pig,* Harmondsworth Middlesex, Puffin Books, 1983.

Mathews, Freya, *For love of matter: A contemporary panpsychism*, New York, SUNY, 2003.

_____, *Reinhabiting reality: Towards a recovery of culture*, New York, SUNY, 2005.

_____, 'Vale Val,' *Environmental values,* Vol. 17, 2008, pp. 317–321.

Merchant, Carolyn, *The death of nature: Women, ecology and the scientific revolution*, London, Wildwood House, 1980.

Midgley, Mary, *Animals and why they matter*, London, Penguin, 1983.

Moriarty, Paul Veatch, & Mark Woods, 'Hunting ≠ Predation', *Environmental ethics*, Vol. 19, Winter, 1997.

Noske, Barbara, *Humans and other animals*, London, Pluto Press, 1989.

Palmer, J., *50 Key thinkers on the environment*, London, Routledge, 2001.

Plumwood, Val, *Feminism and the Mastery of Nature*, London, Routledge, 1993.

_____, 'Androcentrism and Anthrocentrism: Parallels and Politics', *Ethics and the Environment* Vol. 1 No. 2, 1996, pp. 119–152.

_____, *Environmental Culture: The Crisis of Reason,* London, Routledge, 2002.

_____, 'Being Prey', in *Terra Nova*, Vol. 1, No. 3 Summer 1996, pp. 32–44.

_____, 'Towards a Progressive Naturalism', in T. Heyd ed. *Recognizing the autonomy of nature*, New York, Columbia University Press, 2005, pp. 25–53.

_____, 'The concept of a cultural landscape', *Ethics and the environment*, Vol. 11, No. 2, 2006, pp. 115–50.

_____, 'Journey to the heart of stone,' in *Culture, creativity and environment: New environmentalist criticism*, eds. F. Beckett and T. Gifford, Amsterdam, Rodopi, 2007, p. 17.

_____, 'Review of Deborah Bird Rose's *Reports from a wild country*,' *Australian humanities review*, Vol. 42, 2007.

_____, 'The cemetery wars: Cemeteries, biodiversity and the sacred,' *Local–Global: identity, security and community*, Vol. 3. Special issue: Exploring the legacy of Judith Wright, eds. Martin Mulligan and Yaso Nadarajah, 2007, pp. 54–71.

_____, 'Nature in the active voice,' *Australian humanities review*, Vol. 46, 2009, pp. 113–129.

Robbins, John, *Diet for a new America*, Walpole, N.H, Stillpoint, 1987.

Rose, Deborah Bird, *Nourishing terrains: Australian Aboriginal views of landscape and wilderness*, Canberra, Australian Heritage Commission, 1996.

_____, *Reports from a wild country*, Sydney, University of New South Wales Press, 2004.

Snyder, Gary, *The practice of the wild*, New York, North Point Press, 1990.

Waller, David, 'A vegetarian critique of deep and social ecology', *Ethics and the environment*, Vol. 2 No. 2, 1997, pp. 187–198.

Wittgenstein, Ludwig, *Philosophical investigations*, Oxford, Blackwell, 1954.

Made in the USA
Monee, IL
08 April 2024

56554292R00063